from fear
to
LOVE

from fear
to
LOVE

OVERCOMING

THE BARRIERS

TO **HEALTHY**

RELATIONSHIPS

RAY & NANCY KANE

MOODY PUBLISHERS
CHICAGO

All Scripture quotations, unless otherwise indicated, are taken from the *Holy Bible, New International Version*®. NIV®. Copyright © 1973, 1978, 1984 by International Bible Society. Used by permission of Zondervan. All rights reserved.

Scripture quotations marked TLB are taken from *The Living Bible* copyright © 1971. Used by permission of Tyndale House Publishers, Inc., Wheaton, Illinois 60189. All rights reserved.

Library of Congress Cataloging in Publication Data

Kane, Raymond A.
From fear to love / by Raymond A. Kane, Nancy J. Kane
p. cm.
Includes bibliographical references.
ISBN-10: 0-8024-3087-2
ISBN-13: 978-0-8024-3087-8
1. Love—Religious aspects—Christianity. 2. Fear—Religious aspects—Christianity. I. Kane, Nancy J. II. Title

BV4639 .K36 2002
241´.4—dc21

We hope you enjoy this book from Moody Publishers. Our goal is to provide high-quality, thought-provoking books and products that connect truth to your real needs and challenges. For more information on other books and products written and produced from a biblical perspective, go to www.moodypublishers.com or write to:

Moody Publishers
820 N. LaSalle Boulevard
Chicago, IL 60610

7 9 10 8 6

Printed in the United States of America

To Eric and Krista,

You are the greatest gifts

we could have ever received.

Contents

FOREWORD

*I*n one of our favorite films, *The Shawshank Redemption,* Ellis Boyd "Red" Redding (played by Morgan Freeman) tells the story of Andy Dufresne. Andy is a young, successful banker wrongly convicted of murdering his wife in 1947 and sentenced to two consecutive life terms at Shawshank Prison.

Halfway through the film, an old con, Brooks Hadlin, becomes enraged and threatens to take another inmate's life, holding a makeshift knife at the inmate's throat. A few tense moments later, Red and Andy persuade Brooks to lay down his knife. That's when they discover that Brooks had just received word that his parole was finally approved. The mere thought of freedom outside the prison walls after fifty years of being locked up is enough to send Brooks over the edge.

Later, discussing the incident in the prison yard, an inmate concludes that Brooks had gone mad. Red quickly disagrees: "Brooks ain't no bug! He's just . . . institutionalized." Red goes on to say that if a man has been in prison for fifty years as Brooks has, it becomes all he knows. "In here, he's an important man," Red says. "He's an educated man. Outside, he's nothing, just a used-up con with arthritis in both hands." He then describes the fear and dread of a man who trembles at the thought of leaving a prison. Finally he tells the other inmate:

"You believe whatever you want . . . but I'm telling you, these walls are funny. First you hate them, then you get used to them. Enough time passes . . . you get to depend on them."

Truth be told, many of us are like Brooks Hadlin. We have confined ourselves and our relationships within the walls of familiarity. We know that something better—something more exciting, vibrant, and real—is beyond our borders, but fear gets the better of us and we opt for what we know rather than what could be.

Fear locks us into friendships, family relationships, and even marriages that aren't what we intended. Fear restricts relationships to a prison that allows love only an occasional visit.

But here's good news: The book you hold in your hands provides the key to unlocking your prison of fear. Maybe you've been burned in a relationship and fear being burned again. And you gotten used to this fear as time has passed. Maybe you are beginning to depend on your fear; it now keeps you from even trying. That's understandable. The prison walls of fear are funny that way. But you no longer need to confine yourself and your relations to only the familiar.

From Fear to Love provides a better way. You can overcome the barrier of fear and find love like you've never known before. Ray and Nancy Kane show you how. Through this helpful book, they will guide you, step by step, beyond the stark prison walls of fear and walk with you toward healthy relationships that enjoy the luxurious freedom of love

DRS. LES AND LESLIE PARROTT
Seattle Pacific University

ACKNOWLEDGMENTS

A good friend of ours, Kevin Miller, compared the creative process of writing a book to being in the last stages of labor of giving birth. Initially we thought his description was a bit dramatic; now we realize it is truer than we ever imagined. This work has truly been a "labor" of love. There have been so many people that have helped in the birth process.

Space does not permit us to thank everyone who has helped us along the way. In particular, though, we would like to thank Jim Bell for believing in us and the concept of this book, giving us this wonderful opportunity and opening up a whole new world for us. John Aiello came into our lives when this book was a fragile compilation of diagrams. We are grateful for his wisdom and honesty with the initial stages of this book. Jim Vincent should also be commended for his masterful "cleaning up" of our work to bring it to a level we could have never done on our own.

So many other people have encouraged us along the way. Gloria and Al Allison (Nancy's parents), have been there in all times of need. Larry Tornquist has been a source of great encouragement and steadfast love throughout the stormy seasons of our life. Carol Reed lifted up the "shield of faith" and believed this book would happen when circumstances seemed to indicate otherwise. Sherry and Chris Lajiness showed us love in so many practical and powerful ways when times seemed most hopeless. Mickie O'Donnell, Kevin and Karen Miller, and Nell Thomas were faithful prayer warriors. Their enthusiasm and support has meant so much.

We also want to express our gratitude to the friends and clients who have shared their life stories with us and truly have been our teachers in this process of learning to let go of fear and embrace love.

Introduction:
A Journey Toward Love

A book is truly a reflection of its author. We have experienced our own turbulent journey from fear to love. In moving from a life driven by fear to a life motivated by love, we entered a path we would not have chosen on our own. Given our own preference, we would have chosen to live life unaware, self-indulgent, and ultimately running from our true selves.

Our journey from fear to love began in 1989. Ray was working as a senior vice president for a successful real estate developer in Chicago. He was responsible for designing, developing, marketing, and managing retirement communities. Ray's grandma, whom he adored, instilled in him a love for the elderly. Providing for the needs of people in the twilight of their lives was immensely rewarding for Ray. However, with the rewards of the job came a cost. Due to the magnitude of projects that were being developed, Ray was working sixty to eighty hours per week.

It was easy to rationalize the demands the job was making on our marriage and family. We lived quite comfortably, flew to exotic places where the upscale communities were being built, and rubbed shoulders with the accomplished and successful. Behind this facade of success was a broken marriage and two children starved for affection from their dad. Our children were ages two and four at the time. Ray was gone so much our children stopped asking when their dad would return from his trips.

In fact, one Friday evening Ray came home after being on the road for a week. He plopped down in front of the television to relax and watch the evening news. Just as Ray got settled in his chair, Eric came in wanting to play. Ray talked to him for a few minutes and returned to watch television. Eric, intent on getting time with his dad, walked over, turned off the TV, and stood in front of it. Ray told Eric not to touch the television and turned the TV back on. Eric, not easily dissuaded and being careful not to touch the TV with his hands, slowly bent down and gently turned the TV off with his nose. Eric's behavior spoke volumes of how much he needed his dad to be home.

Ray has always been a man of integrity. Even as the heady aroma of success absorbed him, he would eventually do what was right for his family.

One day, completely unannounced, Ray came home and said, "I made a decision a long time ago that I would never let my career take priority over my marriage and family. I'm quitting this company, and I've secured a contract to manage a retirement community in Ohio. This will give us the income we need plus a slower lifestyle." Shortly thereafter, feeling a bit like the Clampetts in *The Beverly Hillbillies*, we loaded up the car and moved to Cleveland.

Life was wonderful in Cleveland. We had time as a family, we had a good income, and the kids were in good schools. We sold our home in Chicago and contracted to have a home built in Westlake, a Cleveland suburb. Little did we know that our peaceful life was about to get stormy.

The storm warnings began when Nancy contracted an aggressive virus and quickly became seriously ill. She was hospitalized for five days.

The storm hit full force eighteen months later. The representative from the investment company that awarded Ray the contract now canceled it. (Later, Ray heard reports from those who knew the company that the person supervising the retirement project likely received a financial kickback for canceling Ray's contract and awarding it to another company.)

We were left without options or backup income. It was 1990, and the retirement industry was going through a depression. At Ray's level of experience, openings were scarce. The storm seemed to rage all around.

What happened next is recorded in chapter 1, where we take you on our wild ride in which our fears rose and assailed us, and we struggled to recognize our motives and fears and address them in healthy ways. From that experience we learned the lesson of this book: The way out of our fears is to practice unconditional love for each other in a manner that is genuine and supportive.

The hard work of recovering financially and discovering what drove the intensity of our fears, controlling behavior, and anger led each of us on a healing journey of discovery. We learned firsthand the insidious effects of the emotion of fear and realized how profoundly it keeps us from becoming the people we are called to be. We learned too that love is the ultimate antidote to fear. In the following pages we want to share our hard-earned insights about the journey from fear to love.

It's a journey most of us must take. In this book we include stories of people who are in process in the journey. For more than twenty years, we have been able to counsel those seeking love, and their stories are included, though in most cases identities have been disguised to protect their privacy. In some instances, the profiles we have presented are composites. In others, unique biographical details have been either omitted or changed. Their stories show how fear hampers us and love frees us.

Obviously, our journey was not without a lot of sweat and tears. As you journey through the pages of this book, you will see we describe what a real loving relationship looks like as well as how the disabling emotion of fear can become like continual withdrawals from the relationship, with the potential to bankrupt any loving relationship. We've learned personally one of the central themes of this book: When we become afraid, we tend to express ourselves in controlling ways both behaviorally and attitudinally, which then affects our ability to love. The fundamental reason that we try to control people is to get our needs met. When our needs for love are not met to our satisfaction, we then supercharge our fear with anger and seek to control more intensely.

Every single one of us has experienced the need to try to control others. However, we all can make new and different choices to move away from our fears and learn to love others—and ourselves—in more healthy and productive ways. That is the message of *From Fear to Love*.

Our Personal Journey from Fear

Two roads diverged in a wood, and I—
I took the one less traveled by,
And that has made all the difference.

-:-

ROBERT FROST
"THE ROAD LESS TRAVELED"

When Ray lost his contract as manager of a retirement community in suburban Cleveland, it was at one of the worst times possible. With the retirement-community sector in a depression, Ray's level of expertise was limited in demand. We moved back to Chicago without any job prospects. For the next fourteen months we had no steady income; what Ray made in one month in 1990, we made for the whole year in 1991. He worked odd jobs and delivered newspapers. Nancy did temporary office work.

Gradually, everything we had previously valued was stripped away. We lost our home, car, and, of course, our standard of living. Our fears began to intensify. *How would we pay for our basic needs? When would Ray get a job? Would we ever get back on top again? What other crises would occur?* These and hundreds of other questions crossed our minds. This began an eleven-year wilderness experience that would not end until 2001.

Some friends were uneasy with our status of being down on our luck and distanced themselves from us. "You guys are living out my worst nightmare. I am afraid that if I get too close to you, what you are going through will be contagious," one friend said, only somewhat in jest.

At times we thought we would have preferred a serious disease to these severe financial straits. *After all,* we reasoned, *when we are ill, others are able to come alongside, but when we go through financial difficulties, people see us as social lepers.* Not only were they avoiding us, but we were perceived as the cause of our own pain—as if we didn't play the game of life right. One day, for instance, I (Ray) remember someone saying to Nancy, "If Ray wouldn't have made those career decisions, you wouldn't be in the mess you are in now."

I will never forget Nancy's reaction and response. "Whatever lessons Ray had to learn, there were lessons for me to learn also." It meant the world to me that Nancy was giving her full support even though at times it felt like I had failed my family.

During the first jobless year, we were living on groceries donated by friends and family. In our humble circumstances, we were thankful that a few people graciously provided for our needs in ways we could never have imagined.

One unforgettable example took place ten days before Christmas. That evening I was at a meeting and Nancy was getting Krista and Eric, then ages four and six, ready for bed. The doorbell rang. Being home alone and in a new neighborhood, she hesitated a moment before going to answer the door. As she descended the stairs, she heard the front screen door close and a car with a loud muffler pulling out of our driveway. Nancy opened the door and saw an envelope in the doorjamb. To her surprise it contained four $100 bills. Eric and Krista were waiting at the top of the stairs. Nancy spun around and waved in the air what was in the envelope. The three of them started jumping up and down and screaming with excitement. If it wasn't for this provision we wouldn't have been able to have Christmas gifts that year. To this day we still have not been able to figure out who left the money for us that Christmas.

I continued to send out dozens of resumés and pursue every lead I had. We became discouraged, tired, depressed, puzzled, and angry with God. We both questioned why we were in these circumstances when I had made a decision to first quit a well-paying job and move to the Cleveland area for the good of the family and our marriage. In our anguish we would say to God, "We made these decisions so that we could be a close, loving family, and instead You leave us with no hope and afraid for our future." We personally questioned our faith. How could a God who says He loves us leave us in such a place? As we continued this questioning, we sought help—spiritual, social, and financial. We listened to sermon tapes for encouragement, we read our Bibles, and we talked to friends and sought their counsel. We sought out our church for temporary financial support which they graciously gave; later we concluded their interest in us was limited: We received only two phone calls in two years, each asking when we would pay back the loan.

Blow After Blow

During this time we were hit with another blow. Because we were unable to reinvest in a new home, we became liable for a $91,000 capital gains tax which we had no means to pay. For the next ten years the Internal Revenue Service pursued us ruthlessly. We were charged interest daily on the balance we owed. We had liens placed on us, and at one point we had our checking account funds seized.

There is no gracious provision in the tax code for catastrophic circumstances. It was irrelevant to the IRS that we did not have the financial means to pay the tax. We talked to our congressman's assistant, asking what we should do. His advice was that we should both get second jobs to pay back our debt—in spite of the impact it would have on our young children. We chose to work hard in the jobs we did have and live simply.

As time progressed, our tax liabilities continued to grow. Desiring to meet our obligations, we agreed to pay the IRS $900 per month toward the $91,000 debt. This payment only covered the monthly interest that was accruing; it never reduced the principal of what we owed.

Within six months of this payment agreement, Ray broke a vertebra in his back from a fall on a friend's trampoline. He was placed in a back brace for twelve weeks. It took approximately eighteen months for him to fully recuperate. Consequently, we were unable to make the $900 monthly payments we had originally agreed upon. The only option we had at that point was to submit an Offer and Compromise to the IRS, which was a legal provision in the tax code which allowed us to negotiate the total balance of what we owed. After two rejected offers, the IRS forced us into both Chapter 7 and Chapter 13 bankruptcy.

It wasn't just losing a significant income, being out of work for fourteen months, and being hounded by the IRS. The circumstantial stresses just kept coming. It felt like a meteor shower that wouldn't end. In addition to these pressures, new ones appeared:

• We started a counseling center as an arm of an existing not-for-profit agency. However, later someone told us that the agency had violated client confidentiality several times. We could not accept this alleged breach of ethics, so we had to discontinue our relationship with the agency and begin a new practice.

- Nancy had the opportunity to start a new career as a professor. As much as this provided additional support for our financial needs, there was a considerable amount of work involved in preparing for new classes, which added to our daily stress.

- Because of our financial situation and various circumstances, we had to move five times, from a large home we owned to renting a much smaller home.

- Nancy was hospitalized with pneumonia for five days.

- Nancy's father was diagnosed with esophageal cancer.

- Ray's mom was diagnosed with lung cancer.

- A car hit our son.

- A conflict arose with a family member resulting in this person severing the relationship, choosing not to reconcile.

- Both of our children had significant educational challenges during this time.

- One of our children contracted a life-threatening disease.

- During the eleven-year period, the pressure of retiring over $500,000 in debt was sometimes overwhelming.

These are only a portion of the difficult experiences in our eleven-year desert experience. A lot happened between these events that added significantly to our stress and fears.

We know some of you reading our circumstances have had a much harder and possibly longer set of trials and tribulations. Yet we have learned that it isn't the number or the intensity of trials that count; it is how we manage them.

We have often said that life is pain management. The key is how effectively we deal with the pain and stress in our lives; that makes all the difference.

Learning What's Worth Living For

Our circumstances forced us to evaluate what was most important in life and what was truly worth living for. We reminded ourselves that God does stand as a sentinel at the gate of our lives, knowing exactly what comes in. We grew to realize that God is more concerned about our relationship with Him than all of our material and earthly pleasures. He came to bring us life in all of its fullness. He allowed everything we had placed security in to be stripped away, so that we would find security in a way no earthly pleasure could satisfy.

It wasn't our training in psychology that got us through our difficult times; it was our faith in Jesus Christ. The building of faith is a growth process; it requires a long time. God is working from here to eternity to develop each person's faith and to increase his or her capacity to love.

In the Bible we learn how to respond when trials and difficulties come into our lives: We are to "consider it pure joy . . . whenever [we] face trials of many kinds, because . . . the testing of [our] faith develops perserverance" (James 1:2–3). The word *trial* is defined as a test or examination of our character. When trials come, we are to receive them with joy, recognizing a God-given opportunity to identify those specific character flaws we need to change so that we can love more purely.

The purification process for gold requires the fire to become extremely hot so that the impurities will rise to the top. Once these impurities rise, they are scraped off so that the gold remaining will become pure. The trials in our life are like purifying gold. God uses these trials to allow those character issues that are blocking our ability to love to rise to the surface. James is saying that a real sense of contentment and joy develops when we see ourselves becoming who we have been created to be—caring and compassionate people. The trials of our life can either make us or break us. They can make us bitter or better.

When there are national tragedies, when our own personal world crumbles, we are forced to look at what is most important in life and what is worth living for.

What was most important, and the reason why we chose to write this book, is how we managed all the feelings, pain, and fear that seemed to camp out at our front door never wanting to leave. We found ourselves, in the midst of the pressure, reacting in sometimes powerful and destructive ways. Our fears were not only multifaceted but also ran very deep. The different and difficult circumstances brought us face-to-face with fears of failure, abandonment, rejection, and even of death.

During a Barrage of Difficulties . . .

The barrage of difficulties alone caused us to feel fearful that our circumstances would never change. Many times, as a response to the unrelenting pressure, we would be overcome by anxiety and panic. Our minds would race to all the worst possible outcomes. Other times, our fears would turn into anger, wanting to blame others, or harshly condemn ourselves for our circumstances.

The anxiety intensified whenever some people close to us became critical of the decisions we made. We received comments that we had not been wise in manageing our finances, and that is what caused our circumstances. Others deduced that we should have had a larger amount of assets before Ray took the contract to oversee the facility in Cleveland. It seemed difficult for them to realize that we were in circumstances that were out of our control. At a time when we were most vulnerable, their critical judgments hurt deeply. Further, we felt abandoned by others we knew, who were uncomfortable with our being "down on our luck" and preferred not being around us.

As husband and wife, we even felt deserted at times by each other. The feelings of desertion were most intense when our fears were the most overwhelming and we were unable to see any hope for deliverance. When we were both equally overwhelmed by our circumstances, it was difficult to comfort each other.

And we admit that we each struggled with depression. At one point, Ray became seriously depressed and moved into despair. He became overwhelmed by the intensity of the stress and the hopelessness of our circumstances changing. As a provider for the family, he felt heartbreak seeing all that he had worked hard to gain be lost so quickly. What compounded the pain was knowing it would take a long time to save again for our children's education, a home, and retirement.

Our powerful fears of what was happening to us intensified our conflicts. Little situations that normally would not bother us would suddenly become grounds for a heated debate. If either one of us perceived the other as being critical or demanding and therefore not "safe," we would immediately lash out at the other. When we feel most vulnerable, it is those closest to us that often feel the impact of our defensive, self-protective behavior.

A Unique "Dance" of Fear and Control

When both people in a relationship try to control each other, conflict inevitably results. We then develop a "loop" or dance as a way to deal with the negative feelings that result.

Whenever a painful or fear-producing event would disrupt our lives, we would both react by becoming controlling. The issues for discussion were different, but our unhealthy ways of dealing with fear, anger, and control were the same. Even though we were trained therapists, we were not exempt from creating our own unique dance. We found that our personal loop was not much different from those we counseled. Ray would control by moving into a hyper-focus mode to try to solve the problem. Nancy would also move into this mode, and if she disagreed with a solution Ray was wanting to implement, she would try to control Ray to do it differently. Ray in turn would become defensive and try to boost his position by getting angry while feeling inside that Nancy just wasn't understanding what he was trying to do. Nancy would react to Ray's anger and feel hurt that he wasn't hearing her view.

Simply put, we would both act like pit bulls on a bone, not letting go of what we thought was right.

Throw almost any issue into our loop or interaction, and we would play out our roles well. It took a lot of energy and willingness to look honestly at ourselves in order to understand why we got so angry and controlling with each other. For many couples, staying stuck in their loop of fear, anger, and control can be intense. (Later chapters will look at just how intense it can become.) It is as if their relationship takes on the drama of a World Wrestling Federation match.

Eventually, out of pure survival, we knew we needed to try and find the underlying causes of the tension between us. Here is what we found. Under Ray's anger and controlling behavior, a deep fear "dwelt" that our situation would get worse. Somehow he believed that if he moved into a controlling mode, he could reduce the level of stress for himself. In my strong reaction to Ray's anger, I could neither problem-solve with him nor be objective. The reason? I wrongly perceived his display of anger as showing disrespect. Each reaction was defensive, and instead of working at communicating and listening to each other, we protected our own selves.

Once we became aware that it was the various fears that were fueling our anger and causing us to control, we both decided that we would work hard at telling each other when we were afraid rather than react defensively. Sometimes when one of us was deep into our own anxiety, the other tried, and was sometimes successful, at highlighting those fears that were attempting to rear their ugly heads. As we recognized this "dance of fear" we were engaged in, we made a decision that because we were in the same foxhole we would make every effort to keep our guns pointed outside rather than at each other.

Taking Responsibility, Loving Unconditionally

We decided to take personal responsibility for our own actions and identify our fears as they arose. The result? We were able to become less angry, defensive, and controlling and thus we were able to experience each other's loving support. Most important, we became freer to unconditionally love each other in a manner that we both felt was genuine and supportive.

Without question, this was the single most important paradigm shift we ever made. Nancy and I resolved to work toward understanding what God wanted to teach us rather than lamenting over what we lost and further blaming each other for our circumstances. Second, we remained committed to growing and taking personal responsibility for our actions and attitudes. Of course, many times we drifted away from that perspective. Nevertheless, we worked hard to maintain our focus by staying connected to each other and working together to manage our difficulties.

When fears arise in *all* of our lives, let us recognize and resist the temptation to numb our feelings by seeking wealth, prestige, power, or beauty. We need to define who we are and what is truly important. Remember, our lives must be directed by what wealth, prestige, and power can never gain—loving others and being grateful for the life God has given us.

It is hard to describe what happens when a heart begins to transform and embrace the notion that life is really about learning how to love more purely. For the two of us—and for you—character flaws will always be exposed under pressure, just as the purity of our hearts will shine when trials come our way. God is always most interested in the building and developing of our character. He wants more than anything for us to love Him, worship Him, and grow to love others more purely. In *From Fear to Love,* join us as we learn to turn our fears to love, so that we may care for others more freely and fully.

Love: The Antidote to Fear

Fear not that your life shall come to an end, but rather it shall never have a beginning.

❖

JOHN HENRY NEWMAN

Addressing the topic of love is like trying to capture air in a bottle. You know it's there but you can't see it or touch it, and it's extremely difficult to gather. We all try at times to put words to those elusive feelings that give us that warm sensation around the heart and make our arms want to hug. Thousands of books have been written about love—our need for it, even our addiction to it, and the pain it creates when we don't receive it.

In addition, thousands of poems and songs have been written with love as their theme. Individually we place much of our attention and energy toward falling in love, finding love, and staying in love. Despite all this, it seems that many of us really don't know what love is.

A friend once passed along to us a list of wise sayings—

except this list was from children. Children were asked to share their definitions and opinions on love. Here are a few notables:

- "Love will find you even if you're trying to hide from it. I've been trying to hide from it since I was five, but the girls keep finding me" (Dave, age eight).
- "I'm not rushing into love. Fourth grade is hard enough" (Regina, age ten).
- When people are in love they act "Mushy . . . like puppy dogs . . . except people don't wag their tails so much" (Arnold, age ten).

Children have a way of cutting to the core of things. They have a way of addressing the simplicity of what we as adults make incredibly complex.

What Love Is

Somewhere along the way we have lost the real meaning of love. In the same breath that we say we love hot dogs or our car, we also say we love our spouse or friend. There doesn't seem to be a clear definition as to what love really is. It is little surprise that we live in a world where people are hungry for affection and love when we so poorly define it.

Making a Sacrifice

While we have difficulty defining love, we all recognize it when we see it in action. The story of Liza vividly portrays love in a dynamic way. Years ago a little girl named Liza was in a local hospital with a rare and serious disease. To survive, she needed a blood transfusion from someone who had previously conquered the same illness and had developed antibodies for it. Her five-year-old brother qualified as a donor, but everyone was hesitant to ask him since he was just a child. Finally, they agreed to have the doctor pose the question.

The attending physician tactfully asked the boy if he was willing to be brave and donate blood for his sister. Though he didn't understand much about such things, the boy hesitated for only a moment before taking a deep breath and saying, "Yes, I'll do it if it will help Liza."

He lay down in a bed beside his sister, and the transfusion began. Dan Millman, a hospital volunteer, tells what happened next:

> [He] smiled, as we all did, seeing the color return to her cheeks. Then his face grew pale and his smile faded. He looked up at the doctor and asked with a trembling voice, "Will I start to die right away?"
>
> Being young, the boy had misunderstood the doctor; he thought he was going to have to give her *all* his blood.[1]

The boy thought he was giving up his life. But he was willing. That boy's sacrificial love, demonstrated by his immediate response to help his sister, touches a chord in our hearts which says, "Would I have been willing to do that?"

Focusing Beyond Our Own Interests

We are able to love like this only when we have checked our fears at the door of our own self-protection. This young boy was not focused on his own interests; he was willing to set those aside for what was best for his sister. When we become focused only on our own interests, we immediately block our opportunity to reach out and touch the needs of those around us.

The love we are called to evidence involves sacrificing our own needs, accepting another person unconditionally, and giving of our time and talents for the good of someone else.

Jesus was asked by the religious rulers of His day what the greatest commandment was. He responded by saying, "'Love the Lord your God with all your heart and with all your soul and with all your mind.' This is the first and greatest commandment. And the second is like it, 'Love your neighbor as yourself'" (Matthew 22:37–39). Jesus was saying that the most significant thing we can do in this world is to love. In addition, love is always expressed in relationships—with God, with others, and with ourselves.

When we choose to love others, we become for them that cold glass of water on a hot day. When we love, we draw out those who are afraid and have become myopically focused on their circumstances and themselves, unable to see hope. Love draws the fear out of our overwhelming circumstances, like ointment that draws the pain out of a sunburn.

A Premier Description

In perhaps the premier description of love, 1 Corinthians 13, the apostle Paul explains the need for and definition of love:

> If I gave everything I have to poor people . . . but didn't love others, it would be of no value whatever
>
> Love is very patent and kind, never jealous or envious, never boastful or proud, never haughty or selfish or rude. Love does not demand its own way. It is not irritable or touchy. It does not hold grudges and will hardly even notice when others do it wrong. It is never glad about injustice, but rejoices whenever truth wins out. If you love someone you will be loyal to him no matter what the cost. You will always believe in him, always

expect the best of him, and always stand your ground in defending him. (vv. 3–8 TLB)

Paul clearly identifies the various qualities and dimensions of love. He reminds us that nothing else really matters as much as loving those around us. To love is to act in the best interest and welfare of someone else. That means developing a passion and commitment to being a truth seeker, truth finder, and truth teller. It also means being people who are able to rise above our own self-absorption in order to see what is best for another.

Becoming Truth Seekers and Tellers

We become truth seekers when we are committed to honestly look at ourselves to see how willing we are to unconditionally love others. It is easy to believe in something yet not be willing to put our beliefs in action. We can easily deceive ourselves about the selfishness in our own souls. We can spend a lifetime blaming others for our own unhappiness and never take responsibility for the times we have created our own misery by waiting for others to love us.

We become truth finders by shining the light of truth on our ill intentions and negative attitudes. Any negative perspective, left unattended, will always multiply and crowd out our ability to freely love. The hurts of the past, if buried alive, will always come back to haunt us in the present moment. Perhaps we have been deeply hurt by someone and have chosen to close off our hearts. If we do not resolve those hurt feelings, we will project them onto new relationships and repeat the past. To live a life of love is to honestly look at ourselves.

As we become truth seekers and truth finders, we are able to be truth tellers. Jesus addressed this in Matthew 7:3–5 when He told His listeners to remove the "plank[s]" from their own eyes so they would be able to identify the "speck[s]" in others' eyes. As we address areas in our own lives that need to be changed, we are more able to enter the lives of others with humility and compassion. When we are committed to the best and highest interest of another, we will become truth tellers—those willing to highlight the areas in others that may be hindering them from becoming all of who God desires them to be.

To be a truth teller is to love others to such a degree that you are willing to sacrifice your own self-interests to help someone else grow to love others and God more deeply.

Overcoming Our Fears

Liza's brother also shows us another aspect of love—the ability to overcome fear. As he faced the fear of his own death, he was able to make a heroic choice that saved Liza's life. This young boy was able to overcome his own fear of dying by choosing to love his sister and display the genuine love that the apostle Paul wrote about in 1 Corinthians 13.

The movement from our fears to living a life of love is not for those who are faint of heart. It takes courage to face our fears and resolve to grow. For some of us, rather than conquering our fears, we have found our fears conquering us. At times, we have experienced our fears like a megaphone in our ears, drowning out that which is good, true, and beautiful in the world.

The Scripture says, "Perfect love drives out fear" (1 John 4:18). Love *is* the antidote to fear. When those we value love us, we grow in our own self-acceptance and personal respect. When we combine the healthy love of others and self-respect for ourselves with the unconditional love God has for each one of us, we are empowered to conquer the fears of our lives. We are then empowered to love with great freedom and joy.

What Love Does

Love is expressed not only in our feelings but in our actions as well. When we choose to generously love others and let go of our fears, we become ambassadors of God's love to the world around us.

Love Touches Our Loneliness

Each of us senses within that we were created to be in relationship with others and not to be left alone. When we love, we are willing to reach out to the lonely and brokenhearted. We are willing to provide that special touch, word of affirmation, or act of kindness . . . to the latchkey child left home alone after school, the adolescent who doesn't have a friend in the world, the wife who feels emotionally abandoned by her husband, or the senior adult who is retired and out of life's mainstream.

When we love as God has called us to, we are willing to tenderly touch those who are weak and vulnerable. Jean Vanier, founder of scores of residential communities around the world for adults with wide-ranging developmental disabilities, wrote about this tender touch in one letter to his coworkers:

> Tenderness implies a deep desire to avoid hurting or harming a weak person. Tenderness is humble; it is an attentiveness, a listening to what a person is saying. . . . Tenderness or gentleness also implies touch: a way of touching another with respect and in truth, a touch that helps the person realise that she is loved and appreciated; a touch which gives support and security. It is different from a possessive touch that tends to depreciate another, preventing his growth to freedom. Tenderness is the opposite of aggressiveness in words or gestures. Tenderness

implies an inner strength, which allows us to love others in truth. Tenderness does not mean simply "being nice" which can be a way of hiding our fear of conflict; it means being truthful in all things. Tenderness teaches us to be true. . . .

In contrast to this world of tenderness or gentleness exists the world of cruelty, where people refuse to welcome others, where there is a lack of consideration and kindness towards others.[2]

We are always in relationship with each other. As we enter into relationships and choose to connect with others, we shine the light of love in their lives. The moon is not our source of light; it only reflects the light of the sun. In the same way, we are to reflect God's love to those around us.

English poet John Donne declared this truth memorably in his *Devotions upon Emergent Occasions:*

The church is . . . universal, so are all of her actions; all that she does belongs to all. When she baptizes a child, that action concerns me; . . . when she buries a man, that action concerns me; all mankind is of one author, and is one volume. . . . No man is an island, entire of itself; every man is a piece of the continent, a part of the main. If a clod be washed away by the sea, Europe is the less, as well as if a promontory were . . . ; any man's death diminishes me, because I am involved in mankind, and therefore can never send to know for whom the bell tolls; it tolls for thee.[3]

When the Christian community as a whole grabs hold of this notion that we are all connected to each other, we will find people meeting each other in ways that strengthen those in pain to meet the challenges of each day.

We need each other to not only survive but thrive in this

world. The redwood trees of California are the largest living things on the face of the earth. By their size and stature, it would appear they could stand on their own, independent of one another. This is not the case. Redwood trees have very shallow root systems. So how do they stand and support their size? They grow in groves where their roots intertwine and quite literally support one another and become a mighty forest.

Conversely, when people feel a lack of connection with others, it affects them in ways that threaten their very survival. One Swedish study followed the lives of more than 17,000 men and women between ages twenty-nine and seventy-four for six years. Researchers found those who were the most lonely and isolated had almost four times the risk of dying prematurely during this period.[4] In another study of elderly men living in Sweden, those who had a low availability of emotional support or who lived alone had more than double the premature death rate of the other men, even after controlling for other factors that influence disease. The study indicated, "Those who lacked social ties were at increased risk of dying from coronary heart disease, stroke, cancer, respiratory diseases, gastrointestinal diseases, and all other causes of death."[5]

The expression "to die of a broken heart" is truer than most of us care to realize. We quite literally shorten our physical span of life by not living lives characterized by intimate relationships. Indeed, we survive by staying connected in meaningful, loving relationships with each other.

Love Speaks Words of Affirmation

A powerful way to put our love into action is to speak words of affirmation to those we love. Words of affirmation are like a fresh spring of water, nurturing and restoring our souls. When we affirm others, we identify that which is good and beautiful in them. It is bringing to their attention what they may not even see in themselves. We all long to be encouraged and loved.

In a recent issue of *Reader's Digest,* the author challenged readers:

> Try to name the five wealthiest people in the world. Name the last five winners of the Miss America competition. Name ten people who have won the Nobel or Pulitzer Prize. Now, name three friends who have helped you through a difficult time. Name five people who have taught you something worthwhile. Think of a few people who have made you feel appreciated and special. The people you'll never forget are not the ones with the most credentials, the most money, or the most awards. The people who make a difference in your life are the ones who care. And they will live forever.[6]

How often have you felt discouraged and recalled some words of encouragement from a coach, teacher, parent, or someone special? Or perhaps you received a reassuring word from someone you admired, who said you could achieve your dreams. We all long to be told what makes us exceptional. We all desire to be told what others see as good and valuable in us. To have words of affirmation poured into our soul gives us the energy to run the distance of life's journey before us but also gives us the strength to manage life's daily struggles.

It is when we haven't received these words of affirmation and statements of character as children that we become adults with a deep sense of emptiness. Ray and I have worked with countless individuals who have wept over never hearing words they longed to hear from a spouse, parent, or friend. They include daughters who spent their lives waiting to hear their dads tell them they were loved, husbands who longed to hear their wives express appreciation for their hard work and provision, and wives who longed to hear their husbands simply say, "I love you."

Love's Affirming Words Grant Value

Part of what it takes to develop a healthy self-esteem and to have the personal fortitude to handle life's difficulties means that at one time or another we needed to have a person or people pour into our souls statements and affirmations that identified what was good in us as individuals. We can encourage others to become whole people through our words of blessing. In his book *Life of the Beloved,* Henri Nouwen, who served as a priest for a community of mentally handicapped adults, described one encounter with the power of affirmation in others' lives.

Shortly before I started a prayer service in one of our houses, Janet, a handicapped member of our community, said to me: "Henri, can you give me a blessing?" I responded in a somewhat automatic way by tracing with my thumb the sign of the cross on her forehead. Instead of being grateful, however, she protested vehemently. "No, that doesn't work. I want a real blessing!" I suddenly became aware of the ritualistic quality of my response to her request and said, "Oh, I am sorry, . . . let me give you a real blessing when we are all together for the prayer service." She nodded with a smile, and I realized that something special was required of me. After the service, when about thirty people were sitting in a circle on the floor, I said, "Janet has asked me for a special blessing. She feels that she needs that now." As I was saying this, I didn't know what Janet really wanted. But Janet didn't leave me in doubt for very long. As soon as I had said, Janet has asked me for a special blessing she stood up . . . and walked toward me. I was wearing a long white robe with ample sleeves covering my hands as well as my arms. Spontaneously, Janet put her arms around me and put her head against my chest. Without thinking, I covered her with my sleeves so that she almost vanished in the folds of my robe. As we held each other, I said, "Janet, I want you to know that you are God's Beloved Daughter. You are Precious in God's eyes. Your beautiful smile, your kindness to the people in your house and all the good things you do show us what a beautiful human being you are. I know you feel a little low these days and that there is some sadness in your heart, but I want you to remember who you are: a very special person, deeply loved by God and all the people who are here with you."

As I said these words, Janet raised her head and looked at me; and her broad smile showed that she had really heard and received the blessing. When she returned to her place, Jane, another handicapped woman, raised her hand and said, "I want a blessing too." She stood up and, before I knew it, had put her face against my chest. After I had spoken words of blessing to her, many more of the handicapped people followed, expressing the same desire to be blessed. The most touching moment, however, came when one of the assistants, a twenty-four-year-old student, raised his hand and said, "And what about me?" "Sure," I said. "Come." He came, and, as we stood before each other, I put my arms around him and said, "John, it is so good that you are here. You are God's Beloved Son. Your presence is a joy for all of us. When things are hard and life is burdensome, always remember that you are loved with an everlasting love." As I spoke these words, he looked at me with tears in his eyes and then he said, "Thank you, thank you very much."[7]

We see so clearly the power of Nouwen's words to be a balm of healing and hope. Nouwen's words communicated to the residents as well as the staff the love he felt for them and their unique contribution to their community. We all need to be reminded of our value. We need to hear that our presence makes a difference in this world. As Pastor Nouwen did, we too often underestimate the value of our words and actions.

As a husband and wife team, we have spoken often of the power of affirmation in the workshops we have conducted. On occasion, we have asked if anyone could remember when a significant person had given them words of affirmation. As we would look across the room, we would see everyone working hard to retrieve those words of affirmation that had been spoken to them. Those who could remember the tender words recalled how they felt encouraged, trusted, and believed in for their gifts and talents. As they shared their stories, we could hear the warm tone in their voices reflecting the love they felt as those affirming words of affirmation fell upon them.

Love's Affirming Words are Life Changing

Ray had one of those moments with a close friend. It was life changing. A few years ago, Ray went to visit his father's grave; it was the twenty-fifth anniversary of his death. During the difficult years of his dad's alcoholism and death, a dedicated youth leader, Dave Veerman, had come alongside Ray's family. Then, more than two decades later, Dave accompanied Ray to his dad's grave. Dave tenderly listened as Ray shared his pain and sorrow.

After their time together, just as Dave turned to say good-bye, he looked Ray in the eyes and said, "You're a good man, Ray." Ray walked away, got in his car, broke down, and wept.

No one had ever affirmed him like that. Ray's father, because of his pain, was never able to come out of himself long enough to recognize and affirm Ray or his two brothers. Dave's words to Ray were life changing. Words can be incredibly powerful when spoken in truth and love.

How Love Heals

Many of us can think of times when a simple act of kindness from someone felt like a cup of cold water on a hot day. Years ago, Elizabeth Ballard of Chesapeake, Virginia, described the ongoing relationship between a young boy named Teddy Stallard and his teacher, Miss Thompson, that powerfully depicts how love can have a lasting impact on someone's life.

At the start of each school year, Miss Thompson would greet her students with the same words. "Boys and girls, I love you all the same. I have no favorites." Yet Miss Thompson knew this wasn't entirely true; she liked some more than others. Teddy Stallard was not on her "like" list, perhaps because of his generally sullen responses. When Miss Thompson would call on him, he would respond with only "yeah" or "no." He appeared as if he were long overdue for a good shower. His clothes were wrinkled and smelled stale.

When she marked his papers, she found a certain twisted satisfaction in writing "F" at the top. Yet Miss Thompson was a seasoned teacher, and she should have known about Teddy from his school records.

First grade: Teddy shows promise with his work and attitude, but poor home situation.

Second grade: Teddy is a good boy, but he is too serious for a second grader. His mother is terminally ill.

Third grade: Teddy is becoming withdrawn and detached. His mother died this year. His father shows no interest.

Fourth grade: Teddy is a troubled child. He needs help.

Now in the fifth grade, Teddy joined in when the class had their Christmas celebration. The students put their gifts on Miss Thompson's desk and waited eagerly for her to open them. All the presents were nicely wrapped in holiday colors except for the one from Teddy. His gift was in plain brown wrapping. As she opened Teddy's present, out dropped two gifts: a shabby rhinestone bracelet with stones missing and a partly empty bottle of cheap perfume.

Tony Campolo, who retells Elizabeth Ballard's story in his book *Let Me Tell You a Story*, explains what happened next:

> The other children giggled at the shabby gifts, but Miss Thompson had enough sense to snap on the bracelet and take some perfume out of the almost-empty bottle and put it on her wrist. Holding her wrist up to the other children, she said, "Isn't it lovely?" The other children, taking their cue from the teacher, all agreed.
>
> At the end of the day when all the other children had left, Teddy came over to her desk and said softly, "Miss Thompson . . . all day today you smelled just like my mother used to smell. That's her bracelet you're wearing. It looks very nice on you. . . . I'm really glad you like my presents." After he left, she got down on her knees and buried her head in her hands and cried and cried and cried, and she asked God to forgive her.
>
> The next day when the children came to class, they had a new teacher. It was still Miss Thompson, but she was a new teacher. She cared in ways that the old teacher didn't. She reached out in ways that the old teacher didn't. She reached out to all the children, but especially to Teddy. She nurtured them and encouraged them and tutored them when they needed extra help. By the end of that school year Teddy had caught up with a lot of children. He was even ahead of some.[8]

Though Miss Thompson kept track of Teddy for some time after he left her class, eventually he moved away and Miss Thompson lost contact. Years later a note appeared in her school mailbox:

Dear Miss Thompson:

I am graduating from high school. I wanted you to be the first to know.

Love,

Teddy Stallard

Other notes followed from Teddy at each major life event: a note expressing delight in graduating from the university (he graduated second in his class), another note sharing the joy and relief of finishing medical school. It ended with an invitation:

Dear Miss Thompson:

I'm going to be married, the 27th of July to be exact. I want you to come and I want you to sit where my mother would have sat. You're the only family I have now. Dad died last year.

Love,

Teddy Stallard

Miss Thompson went and sat in the front of the church. She sat where Teddy's mother would have sat ... because she was worthy of that honor.[9]

Teddy Stallard showed his ability to love by reaching out to Miss Thompson in sharing his mother's perfume and jewelry. His risk brought healing power not only for himself but for Miss Thompson as well. When we love in this way, we become the balm for the wounds of others' souls.

Dr. Dean Ornish, author of *Love and Survival,* writes,

Love and intimacy are at the root of what makes us sick and what makes us well, what causes sadness and what brings happiness, what makes us suffer and what leads to healing. If a new drug had the same impact, virtually every doctor in the country would be recommending it for their patients. It would be malpractice not to prescribe it—yet with few exceptions, we doctors do not learn much about the healing power of love, intimacy and transformation in our medical training.[10]

We were created to find meaning and love. Our whole being is affected when we are loved. To be loved is to find a purpose for living. Not only does it affect us physically, but we are able to draw on another's belief in us to battle life's hardships.

To make a difference in others' lives, we need to mark our lives by a love that is so dynamic that people around can't help but be drawn to us. We need to evidence a love that is willing to enter into others' lives deeply and sacrificially—love that is marked by genuineness, warmth, and compassion, that values the worth and dignity of each individual.

We have defined what love is, what love does, and how love heals. We have seen how, when we love, we are able to overcome our fears and help others in their fears. When people choose to pour into our lives their love, we receive the emotional energy necessary to manage life's difficulties. Teddy Stallard's courage to reach out and show a simple act of love began a relationship with Miss Thompson that transformed both of their lives forever.

CHAPTER THREE

The Many Faces of Fear in Society

*Men hate each other because they
fear each other; they fear each other
because they don't know each other.*

※

MARTIN LUTHER KING JR.

The old metaphor holds true: Life is a journey. Along the way, we can become anxiety-ridden travelers clinging to familiar places, fearful of meeting people and going to new places. Or we can become bold explorers, venturing out on unexplored paths, discovering newfound territory along the way. We all long for something more from our lives and relationships but are blocked so often by a simple but life-altering four-letter word: *fear.*

The two words we all must deal with in our lives are *fear* and *love.* We long for love but are afraid to take a chance. We want close relationships but are scared that we may be hurt. We are lonely and stress-filled because we are terrified of taking a risk to depend on others. We are held captive by our fear yet want the freedom of love.

It is a bold undertaking to move from a life paralyzed by fear to experiencing love in all of its wonder. "The real voyage of discovery consists not in seeking new landscapes but in having new eyes," explains Marcel Proust. As travelers, we need new eyes to see how we let fear block us from loving, caring relationships.

Our first stop on this journey begins with our need to understand how our world and society contribute to our feeling afraid. We are all citizens of a world community. "Every man is a part and piece of myself, for I am a part and member of mankind," Thomas Merton has said. It is easy for each one of us to think we really aren't affected by our society. The reality is we are more significantly affected than we even realize. A single drop of water doesn't cover much of the ground, but the collection of raindrops in a storm can bring green grass, blooming flowers, or hurricanes of massive destruction. It is also true for each one of us. Collectively, we impact our world for good or evil.

How we, on the whole, deal with fear compels us to take seriously the impact unresolved fears can have on our marriage and family, neighborhood, town, and country. In our society, there are three distinct faces of fear: the face of prejudice, the face of irrationality, and the face of isolation.

Fear as the Face of Prejudice

Being a small boy, Nkosi Johnson was not easy to notice at first. Yet despite his size, he exhorted people to meet their fears head-on, to be courageous, and reach out in love to those who were in desperate need. In a country where families shun those like him and treat them like lepers, Nkosi stood against the merciless attacks of prejudice like a David opposing Goliath.

Nkosi was born in South Africa with the AIDS virus. His mother was too poor to bring him up, so he was adopted when he was three. Somehow, he miraculously outlived most of those born with AIDS. In 2001, at age twelve, Nkosi walked into eternity.

Before his death, Nkosi successfully defied the policies that kept HIV-infected children out of public schools; he countered with reason the panic of school parents who feared contamination of their children. (In fact, one parent threatened to send her child to school wrapped in plastic if Nkosi was allowed to continue to attend.)

A small boy with large brown eyes revealing wisdom beyond his years, Nkosi boldly challenged South Africans to reexamine their fear of those afflicted with AIDS.

In a thin, clear voice of a child unaffected by his own tragedy, he declared, "I think it is time that people start realizing that we all—infected people—are all the same. We are human beings. We are nothing different.

"You can love people," Nkosi said. "You can touch them. You can be their friends. You can look after them. We are all the same. Like I say, people are terrified and it is strange. They [those suffering with AIDS] don't understand people who are terrified."[1]

His winsome manner and courageous spirit endeared him to everyone he met. Classmates described Nkosi as a funny and loving boy. This one boy's life modeled how foolish and damaging our fears can be. Nkosi demonstrated the courage of a hundred lions by standing up against the pressure of a whole nation's fear. Rather than become immobilized by the hate that was hurled at him, he chose to take a daring stand—he chose to love those who feared or even despised him.

Nkosi endured—and defeated—the sinister face of prejudice. "Fear is the offspring of ignorance," someone has said. The parents who vehemently opposed Nkosi entering school were reacting, we believe, out of instinct to protect their children from what they perceived was possible harm.

The Latin root word for *anxiety* is *angustia,* which means narrowness. Nkosi's schoolmates' parents' fear was driven by a "narrowness" of understanding. Their collective ignorance of the nature of the AIDS virus fueled their fear.

Nkosi's courageous life graphically demonstrated the disastrous effects of mass panic on the hearts and minds of its people. Like a forest fire out of control, fear can spread with a similar devastating effect in our society.

In America we have seen such prejudice in our fears of people of other races. Racial fears exhibit themselves in both words and actions that lash out at those different from us. The shunning is based typically on unwarranted fears of some threat to our safety. Like Nkosi's plight in South Africa, those of African, Asian, and Hispanic descent (among others) find themselves either shunned or persecuted based on being a perceived danger to the prevailing society.

For instance, the Asian-American community now stands at 11 million people, growing more than 43 percent during the 1990s.[2] With this rapid growth has also come an increase of hate crimes directed toward them.

John Lee, an Asian-American student at the State University of New York at Binghamton, had friends in his college dorm but also foes on campus. One night he was attacked at school and rushed to the hospital with a skull fracture. As a *Newsweek* reporter explained, the attackers were not local gang members or street thugs looking for money. They were members of the school's wrestling team. Witnesses to the incident in 2000 heard the wrestling team students shout racial slurs at John right before they began to beat him.

In the same year, a fifty-year-old Laotian man in Baltimore, while waiting for a bus, was brutally beaten with a broomstick by two teens. Sin Yen Ling, an attorney with the Asian American Legal Defense and Education Fund states, "We see the backlash as communities and social dynamics change. There is fear on all sides and it's becoming more deadly."[3]

Fear as the Face of Irrationality

The network TV newscasts choose stories to enhance their ratings. We cannot watch for more than a few minutes without being bombarded with the risk of economic recession, the threat of terrorist activity, the hazards of cancer-producing foods, the peril of global warming, and the upheaval of political turmoil. Newspapers and radio broadcasts also profile reports that promote an impending crisis. The media know such stories win ratings and sell papers. Like a fuse burning out because of an electrical surge, such reports of impending disaster can cause us to emotionally blow circuits. We then can draw irrational conclusions about others, ourselves, and our world.

Barry Glassner addressed the scare tactics of the media and its influence on us in *The Culture of Fear: Why Americans Are Afraid of the Wrong Things*. "Television news programs survive on scare," he explained. "On local newscasts, where producers live by the dictum 'if it bleeds, it leads,' drug, crime and disaster stories make up most of the news portion of the broadcasts. Evening newscasts on the major networks are somewhat less bloody, but between 1990 and 1998, when the nation's murder rate declined by 20%, the number of murder stories on network newscasts, increased by 600%."[4]

If we are not intentionally discerning while watching the news, we can easily become anxious and conclude that we are merely seconds from a catastrophe. Leonard Sweet, who follows cultural trends, wrote that the "fear thing" makes us seek greater and greater solutions:

The "Fear Thing" is dominating our need for security. Just look at our cars to see the security issue at work. First we install seat belts. Then we install shoulder belts. Then we build contraptions that put both together. Then we turn the shoulder harness into a boa constrictor that pins us to our seats and doesn't let us move. Then we install air bags. Pretty soon we'll be riding around inside a giant marshmallow.[5]

Inflammatory information can affect us in other irrational ways. On October 19, 1987, otherwise known as Black Monday, investors suffered the worst one-day financial loss in the history of the stock market. The New York Stock Exchange had been experiencing an unprecedented climb, and investors wondered with increasing fear when the profit "balloon" would pop. People had been making fortunes on the incredible surges in the market. Investors' worst fears were realized that day. Stocks lost more than $500 billion in market value, affecting not only American investors but also investors around the world. Observers of the collapse said that "fear was the overriding factor," calling the crash a financial panic.

"It is classic mob psychology that takes over," said Burton Siegel, chief investment officer of Drexel, Burnham, & Lambert Inc. "It feeds on itself."[6] Fear was the all-pervasive undercurrent in the market at the time—fear that the market couldn't get any better and fear that it would fall led to the inevitable mass panic and crash.

Such fear is irrational. It feeds on itself. Often similar fear encourages our children to fear also. As parents, we teach them that the world will not be a better place when they get to be adults or that it is unsafe to drink the water. From us or TV, they hear that the sun will give them cancer and that their school is a dangerous place to be.

Mike Weilbacher, president of the Pennsylvania Alliance for Environmental Education, wrote:

Our children are convinced that the ozone hole will soon fry them, global warming will soon flood them, garbage will bury them alive, and rain forest fires will suffocate them as oxygen vanishes. They believe they will inhabit a planet free of pandas, gorillas, whales, condors, tigers, and just about any creature of majesty or mystery. In fact, many kids are convinced they won't even reach adulthood, for there won't even be an earth by then. When they should be celebrating the beauty of life, they instead are told to mourn its loss. Just as they are being introduced to nature, they are told to bid it farewell. And worse, they are told to hate themselves for wreaking this ecological apocalypse, and even revile us, their parents.[7]

Fear may motivate us to make irrational decisions based on people's ethnic background. Fears based on race often are prejudices, as we saw in the attacks on John Lee and the middle-aged Laotian. But often they also are fears based on a lack of thinking. They're irrational.

For example, Charlo, an African-American college student, has witnessed senseless reactions from others to his presence. "I can't even walk down the streets during the day and I will see white people in their cars suddenly locking their doors." Because of the color of his skin, Charlo is wrongfully judged as someone he truly is not.

Such fear is irrational. It's based on no facts or incomplete facts, not on reason. With limited or no understanding of an ethnic group has come cruel, tragic responses that have been termed "hate crimes."

Individuals who commit horrific hate crimes have many times drawn absurd conclusions about an ethnic group and then act on their fears to protect themselves and others. Out of their perceiving a threat of an ethnic group becoming powerful in our society, they react irrationally.

There is a direct correlation between power and fear. We are terrified of who we believe may dominate us because we fear losing control over our choices and lives.

Abdo Ali Ahmed read the note on his windshield. "We're going to kill all of you [expletive] Arabs." Ahmed, a naturalized American who moved to Fresno, California from Yemen thirty-five years earlier, discarded the message. "Why should I be scared?" he told his wife. "I've never done anything wrong." Two days later, on September 29, 2001, Ahmed, father of eight, was shot to death at his convenience store.[8]

The shocking terrorist attacks of September 11, 2001, that destroyed the Twin Towers at New York City's World Trade Center and damaged the Pentagon awoke an irrational fear within some Americans. Realizing the perpetrators, Muslim extremists who acted in evil ways, all had Arabian features, some began to generalize that all Arab men were terrorists or terrorist sympathizers. The result? In the month following the September 11 attack, there were 270 reported violent incidents against Arab-Americans, including 5 murders. Ahmed, sadly, was one of those victims of irrational fears of American citizens shaken (and angered) by the attack. In fact, this figure may be low, as many Arab immigrants are reluctant to call the police for fear of bringing more attention to themselves.[9]

Fear as the Face of Isolation

What are the consequences for each of us as we live in a society marked by so much global fear? In many ways, it has led us to become a culture marked by self-absorbed loneliness and distrust of others. If we believe what we see on television and read in the newspapers, behind our neighbor's friendly smile is someone who is dangerous or weird or—if given a chance—will move into our house and steal all of our most valued belongings.

"The things and people we think about, worry about, reflect upon, prepare ourselves for, and spend time and energy on are in large part determined by a world which seduces us in accepting its fearful questions," writes Henri Nouwen.[10] We can spend many hours asking "what if" questions. For instance (to paraphrase Nouwen), you may ask, "What if someone breaks into my house?" "What if I lose my job?" "What if I lose my mate?" "What if this person doesn't like me?" "What if I don't like him?" Some of us move to a more global level with our "What ifs": "What if we go to war?" "What if there is a nuclear holocaust?" "What if global warming increases?"[11] If this line of thinking continued regularly, we might just find ourselves avoiding the world around us, staying inside watching *The Jerry Springer Show*. (Of course, that would not help.)

Those "what if" questions can cause us to isolate ourselves from others because we don't feel they have our best interests at heart. We may soon find our "closest" friends are on the TV instead. Susan Ager, a columnist for the *Detroit Free Press,* wryly states, "We distrust everyone but the chipper weather people on TV, wrong as they are. We know Ally McBeal better than the woman across the street. Americans have built their isolating walls brick by brick for decades, and it won't be simple to break them down."[12] Our self-imposed walls of isolation become a way of protecting ourselves from our fears of danger and pain.

Nouwen adds, "Without fully realizing it, we become anxious, nervous, worrying people caught in the questions of survival: our own survival, the survival of our families, friends, and colleagues, the survival of our church, our country and our world."[13]

When these survival questions become the guiding focus of our lives, we look with some degree of suspicion on genuine close contact with others.

The isolating effect of fear encourages people to find safety in the protection of their own homes. Beyond the television set, the Internet gives many the illusion of connection with the world around them; but in reality, that connection is only one-dimensional. The nuances of face-to-face communication that can be so revealing are often disguised in E-mail and chat rooms. As usage of the Internet has grown, "Americans are spending less time with friends and family, shopping in stores, or watching television, and more time working for their employers at home—without cutting back their hours in the office," says Stanford University professor Norman Nie. Simply stated, "the more hours people use the Internet, the less time they spend with real human beings."[14]

The Internet can be enticing for people to not have to take the risks they need to be in "real" relationships. Sherry Turkle, a professor at MIT's science, technology and society program, explained: "Terrified of being alone, yet afraid of intimacy, we experience widespread feelings of emptiness, of disconnection, of the unreality of self. And here the computer, a companion without emotional demands, offers a compromise. You can be a loner, but never alone. You can interact, but need never feel vulnerable to another person."[15]

At one time we found a sense of belonging and safety in our neighbors and communities, but because of the increasing isolation in our society, that is no longer the case. At one time homes were built with front porches, where families would set aside time after dinner for waving and talking to neighbors. They are largely gone from newer homes, as we have become secluded, fenced in, and protected from the attack of a neighbor's vicious dog or the nosiness of the neighbor next door. We have become a back-porch society, retreating to our back-yards and secluding ourselves from the world around us.

Walls of Loneliness

This movement away from relationships to protective isolation breeds a mind-set that says, *I must always guard myself; if I don't, someone will rob me of everything I have worked hard to achieve.* Sadly, such thinking not only secures us from possible harm but also builds walls of aching loneliness. We live our lives characterized by self-absorbed protection in which we value our safety far more than those we can reach out to love.

Dean Ornish, a medical doctor who has done extensive research on the connection between physical and emotional health, believes many adults suffer from what he calls "emotional and spiritual heart disease," that is, "the profound feelings of loneliness, isolation, alienation, and depression that are so prevalent in our culture with the breakdown of the social structures that used to provide us with a sense of connection and community." This emotional and spiritual heart disease "is, to me, a root of the illness, cynicism and violence in our society."[16]

We don't need a lot of evidence to convince us how damaging fear is for us. The consequences of a lifestyle dominated by fear are bitter and inescapable.

The truth is we need each other. We want to share our joys and sorrows with others. We want to know at the end of the day that there are people who care about what has happened to us, in spite of our protective tendencies.

Our Need for Each Other

As part of the requirements of a group dynamics class Nancy teaches every semester, each student joins a small group made up of other class members. Throughout the course, the college students are asked to write their reactions and observations of their experiences. At the beginning of the semester, the students initially express a great deal of resistance about the idea of being in a group. They write comments like, "I don't have the time for any more relationships." "Why should I get to know these people?" "To be honest, I'm not sure I even like the members in my group!"

At the end of the semester, the students participate in a class debriefing in which each group tells the rest of the class about their individual experiences in their groups. The remarks are consistently positive, such as "You know, I started out not liking this group. I'm kind of surprised, I have become really fond of these people!" Or "I really misjudged some people and realize after getting to know them they weren't like I thought at all." Or "I am really going to miss my group!"

The students' responses demonstrate how being in groups and relating more closely to each other allows us to touch a chord of need in our hearts for understanding, companionship, and care.

Tony Campolo, a speaker and professor at Eastern College in Pennsylvania, tells the story of going to a funeral home to pay his respects to the family of an acquaintance of his. He arrived at the funeral home and by mistake entered the wrong room. Standing all alone in front of the casket was an elderly woman mourning the death of her husband. She appeared so lonely that Tony couldn't bear to leave and decided to stay for the funeral. He drove to the cemetery with the widow.

At the end of the graveside service, as he and the elderly woman were ready to drive away, he finally confessed to her that he had never known her husband. "I thought as much," said the widow. "I didn't recognize you. But it doesn't really matter." She squeezed his arm so hard it hurt. "You'll never, ever, know what this means to me."[17]

We need to know that there is someone there when we are facing our most painful moments. We need assurance, much like a child who wakes up afraid in the middle of the night. Like that child, we need to be comforted by a warm, tender voice that says, "It's all right. I'm here. Don't be afraid."

Solomon wrote about our need for each other in a book of wisdom called Ecclesiastes.

> Two are better than one, because they have a good return for their work: If one falls down, his friend can help him up. But pity the man who falls and has no one to help him up! Also, if two lie down together, they will keep warm. But how can one keep warm alone? Though one may be overpowered, two can defend themselves. A cord of three strands is not quickly broken. (4:9–12).

Enduring the Pain . . . Together

We need each other for strength to live our lives. If we live in isolation and are alone for too long, we can develop a distorted mind-set that sees the world through the lens of our unresolved pain. When we take a brief look at the background of the marginalized teenagers who retaliate on their peers or the disgruntled employee who has a shooting spree on all of his fellow employees, we see a lifestyle of crippling isolation and bitterness.

It is an illusion to think we can survive on our own. When the storms of life hit hard, we need to know there are people around us who can shore us up. We need friends and loved ones to give us perspective when the pressures of life weigh us down.

Two running backs for the Chicago Bears, Gayle Sayers and Brian Piccolo, became roommates and close friends in the late 1960s. Both excellent athletes, their rivalry only brought them closer. They were able to rise above their ethnic differences—Sayers was African-American; Piccolo was white—and support each other. That support became more meaningful when Piccolo was diagnosed with cancer in 1969. Their story was retold in the compelling TV movie, *Brian's Song.*

The aggressive cancer put Piccolo in the hospital several times that '69 season. Sayers would frequently fly to be by the side of his friend as he battled for his life. The two competitors on and off the field fought together to keep the cancer from winning.

When Sayers was named the winner of the George S. Halas award as "the most courageous player in professional football," he invited the Piccolos to sit next to him during the presentation at the annual Professional Football Writer's Banquet in New York. But on the date of the banquet, Piccolo was too sick to attend and too weak to even leave his bed. Pastor and author Charles Swindoll recalls the scene:

> As the lean, muscular black athlete stood to his feet to receive the award amid the resounding applause of the audience, tears began to flow which he could not restrain. . . .
>
> "You flatter me by giving me this award, but I tell you here and now that I accept it for Brian Piccolo. Brian Piccolo is the man of courage who should receive the George S. Halas award. I love Brian Piccolo and I'd like you to love him. Tonight, when you hit your knees, please ask God to love him too."[18]

How often do we see strong competitive people evidence a friendship like this? These two men modeled for us how love can break through fear on a number of fronts—racial boundaries, competitive struggles, and the loss of someone to death. Sayers and Piccolo showed us the beauty and richness of sacrificial love.

This type of love is the reward we receive when we are willing to break through the cultural barriers of fear to reach out and love each other. The story of Brian Piccolo and Gayle Sayers has been passed down through the years and has inspired many to begin taking risks to care for those we may not have ever considered loving. It takes courage and strength to identify and conquer our fears. When we face our fears, we see changes not only in us but also in the world around us.

From Despair to Deep, Satisfying Love

We have seen fear as the face of prejudice, irrationality, and isolation. We have seen how fear can generate stock markets to fall, economies to falter, people to barricade themselves, increasing their own pain and distress.

Despair would be our only choice if we did not have hope that our circumstances could be changed. Many of us have allowed the existing atmosphere of fear in our culture to pull us like sponges sucked by the currents on the bottom of the sea. We find ourselves being tossed back and forth by each breaking news event. We don't have to be influenced so dramatically. There is hope, if we can learn to react differently.

We all have seen people conquer their fears: a fireman who risks his life to save a young child; a widow who conquers her fear of raising her children alone; the leader who chooses to stand for peace rather than support acts of violence. We can also think of fathers who have lost their jobs and courageously worked to find new employment. Every day we observe brave people who push through their fears to discover a newfound freedom and excitement on the other side of fear's door. They all inspire us to face our own fears.

Nancy once watched a little girl of preschool age learning how to swim. Her mother stood in the pool with open arms, tenderly encouraging her to jump from the side of the pool into the water. Like a pinball machine, her eyes would frantically dart back and forth from the sight of the deep water to her mother's arms. All of a sudden the little girl grabbed her nose and leaped. What seemed insurmountable to the little girl quickly became a fear that was overcome.

We have all seen children conquer their fears only to go on to the next challenge. Each one of us has within us the simple trust of a child to overcome what we fear most.

In the following pages are principles and perspectives that can help free us from the paralyzing effects of fear so that all of our relationships are marked by a deep and satisfying love. Our hope is that you will catch a vision that your life's deepest longings can be fulfilled and that love you once thought was lost can be found.

CHAPTER FOUR

Components
of Fear

*Fear is one thing. To let fear grab you by
the tail and swing you around is another.*

·:·

KATHERINE PATTERSON

On the evening of October 30, 1938, Orson Welles and his *Mercury Theater on the Air* broadcast an historic dramatization of H.G. Wells's classic story, *The War of the Worlds*. Though the program was introduced as a mere drama, many people turned on their radios in midprogram and thought they heard firsthand accounts of the earth being invaded by an army of extraterrestrial beings. The production opened with a news report of a vast interplanetary attack from Mars; then, with supposed live, on-the-scene reports, the tension built.

The hour-long broadcast brought the most widespread and bizarre terror in American history to that point. Surveys indicated at least a million people became frightened and thousands were panic-stricken after listening to the program or hearing from others who had tuned in.[1]

Hadley Cantril, a Princeton University psychologist, studied the panic immediately after it happened and interviewed people who had been a part of the mass hysteria. One listener, Mrs. Walters, told Cantril, "I kept shivering and shaking. I pulled out suitcases and put them back, started to pack, but didn't know what to take. I kept piling clothes on my baby, took all her clothes out and wrapped her up. Everybody went out of the house except the neighbor upstairs.

"I ran up and banged on his door," Mrs. Walters continued. "He wrapped two of his children in blankets and I carried the other, and my husband carried my child. We rushed out. I don't know why but I wanted to take some bread for I thought that if everything is burning, you can't eat money, but you can eat bread."[2]

Cantril found it puzzling why so many people didn't verify the accuracy of the information they were receiving from their radios. In fact, many took the broadcast so seriously they thought their life was actually coming to an end. A college coed reported, "The girls in the sorority houses and dormitories huddled around their radios trembling and weeping in each other's arms. They separated themselves from their friends only to take their turn at the telephones to make long distance calls to their parents, saying goodbye for what they thought was the last time."[3]

Fear can be all-consuming. The atmosphere of panic consumed even the most intelligent of the listeners to the "War of the Worlds" broadcast. An American Institute of Public Opinion poll taken six weeks after the event indicated that about one of every four listeners to the broadcast (28 percent) believed it was a news bulletin, and of those listeners, 70 percent—1.2 million people—were frightened or disturbed by it.[4] This mass panic vividly illustrates the contagious properties of fear. It also shows us what a paralyzing force it can be in our lives.

Psychiatrists have long assumed that depression is the most

common mental problem in the United States. That assumption is wrong, according to a survey on psychiatric ailments done by the National Institute of Mental Health. The survey results actually showed that anxiety disorders, including phobias, panic disorders, and obsessive-compulsive disorders, are the most widespread psychiatric disorder, afflicting 19 million adult Americans ages eighteen to fifty-four.[5] We will look at how our experiences of the feeling of fear affects us physically and cognitively.

Physical Components of Fear

Flight or Fight

Although most of us may not be aware of our particular fears, most of us can identify when our body tells us we are afraid or anxious. Our bodies have an intricate and sophisticated system of dealing with anxiety. In response to anything we perceive as threatening, whether it is our performance evaluation at work or having an argument with our spouse, our autonomic nervous system responds instinctively to notify the various parts of our body to gear up for "flight or fight." This is our body's way of protecting us from what we perceive as danger.

When confronted with danger, the body sends out two sets of signals to the brain. One set signals information to the cerebral cortex, the thinking part of the brain, to explain in detail the threatening situation. The other set of signals shoots directly to the amygdala, the emotional part of the brain, which sets the fear response in motion. The amygdala gets the body ready for action before the thinking part of the brain can actually understand what is going on.

The amygdala sends out messages to our autonomic nervous system to release two chemicals—adrenaline and noradrenaline—that serve as messengers to the whole body to prepare for danger. These hormones provide our body with a supernatural feeling of strength and gear us up for a defense. Our body responds as if we were readying ourselves for a serious physical attack. When this happens our heart starts to pound, our breathing becomes shallow, we begin to sweat, we can feel jittery, our digestive system shuts down, and our stomach becomes queasy. We experience tight muscles down the back of our neck, across our chest, and in our arms. Our pain response reaction is suppressed in order to prevent discomfort which could prevent us from a quick response.

Extra Energy

We once read a story by inspirational author Norman Vincent Peale of a worker who would walk home fearlessly through a cemetery every night after completing the second shift—as midnight approached. One night the man fell into a newly dug grave and couldn't climb out because of loose soil. Being brave, he put his coat around his shoulders and sat down calmly to wait for the gravediggers to arrive in the morning. A short while later, another man fell into the far end of the open grave and began trying to jump and climb out.

The first man listened to the second man's futile efforts and then said, "Boy, you'll never get out that way."

At the sound of a voice in the darkness, the terrified second man leaped out of the grave and ran away.

Our body becomes energized with extra energy, like the frightened man in the grave. We are able to accomplish things we normally could not under other circumstances.

Ray was a gymnast in high school. He had a tendency to fly off the trampoline during competitions. Everyone wondered why until a team member noticed that Ray bounced higher during the meets, throwing off his timing when performing his tricks. Later Ray would tell family members, "I was so pumped up with adrenaline from the anxiety of the competition that I jumped too high and would soar right off the trampoline."

In its natural survival response, the amygdala makes a split-second determination whether we should fight or flee. If we decide to fight, our fear transforms into anger. Imagine receiving a letter from the Internal Revenue Service stating that they have discovered you owe $10,000 in additional taxes. For most people the initial fear response is panic, followed quickly by anger. Rather than calmly writing out a check for the amount due, most of us begin to fume and will contact the IRS, demanding justification for their claim.

If we decide to "flee," then the best course of action is to move away, physically and/or emotionally, from what is threatening us. If we are on a casual stroll with our friend and see a skunk, our flight reaction kicks in and we run for the nearest shelter.

We can also move into a flight response by emotionally avoiding a situation rather than dealing with it head-on. This particularly occurs when we encounter something we perceive is too risky to face.

Carol loved to shop. One day Jim noticed a bill from their charge card and opened it; he saw that they had reached their limits from purchases Carol had made—without telling him. Jim became furious and shouted at Carol, "Why didn't you check with me on this? You know how hard I have been working to get our bills up to date!"

"Carol, your spending habits are ruining our marriage!" he shouted.

Carol rolled her eyes. "Jim, you just get too worked up over everything. If you had a stressful day, don't take it out on me."

Jim couldn't believe her response. "Carol, you are driving me crazy!"

Carol's response is not uncommon for people who encounter situations that they perceive as overwhelming. Carol went into a "flight" mode by avoiding Jim's feelings of frustration. Although she may have received temporary protection for herself, she has created more frustration in her relationship with Jim.

Cognitive Components of Fear

Why are some of us more prone to feeling afraid? Why do some people jump through the ceiling when they are startled by a loud noise and others barely blink their eyes? There are numerous reasons.

The amygdala records all threatening situations for future reference. It sizes up new situations and determines if the events are similar to something we have experienced in the past. If the situation is similar, the amygdala sends out a full-body alert before we have had time to fully consider what we are experiencing. For those of us who have had a lot of anxiety-producing situations, our amygdala becomes activated more readily.

Role of Our Parents and Relatives

Janice was always on the alert. Her timid voice and shy manner indicated she was on constant watch for possible hazards. As an only child born to a single mother, Janice felt she was born to be her mother's scapegoat. Janice had a gentle and quiet demeanor, while her mother was a strong woman with a violent temper. If there was a problem with their finances, it was because of the burden of raising Janice. If her mother had a bad day at work, it was because she had to come home to Janice.

Janice's mother would often tell her that if she wasn't careful she would leave Janice. As a child, Janice can remember waiting for her mother to come home and feeling her whole body become tense. Some days she would become so sick with anxiety that she would become nauseous. She never knew what would happen when her mother would return. As an adult, Janice was always wary as to potential harm. She even found that she became tense when there was nothing to be anxious about.

Some of us, like Janice, have been raised as children to respond fearfully. Our most powerful role models are our parents. If we had mothers or fathers that were anxious, we were raised to believe that the world is a threatening place. We watch their fear reactions and respond in the same manner until as adults we choose to respond differently. We might have heard messages like, "You can't trust anyone," or "Be prepared for tragedy; it will happen sooner or later." Some of us may have received a laundry list of messages like: "Watch out for germs, strangers, new situations, dogs, and the dark." These messages become powerful motivators, keeping us hypervigilant of our response to the world around us.

Role of Our Perceptions

We also process fear through our perception of what we are experiencing. "There is nothing either good or bad, but thinking makes it so," wrote William Shakespeare. Some of us will watch, at the end of the day, a brilliant-colored sunset and revere its beauty. Others of us will see the same sunset and grumble that the day is over and worry that we haven't gotten enough things done.

How we perceive things is pivotal in how we process fear. A mouse was having a heyday in the guidance office of a local high school. As it ran wildly under desks and chairs, women and students started screaming and running, except, of course, Chuck. A former NFL linebacker, Chuck feared nothing, certainly not mice. Armed with a broom in his hand, he casually strolled in the direction of the brash offender. Chuck cornered the mouse in one of the small offices.

As he lunged toward the mouse with the broom, the mouse leaped toward Chuck and landed on his shoulder. Suddenly the secretaries watched in shock as Chuck let out a horrific scream and ran out of the office, awkwardly slapping at his shoulders and tearing off his jacket.

The secretaries and students saw the mouse as threatening. Chuck, on the other hand, saw the mouse as merely an annoyance —until the mouse leaped directly on him. Now perched squarely on his shoulder, the mouse was a imminent threat. In a split second Chuck's perception changed; the level of danger climbed and his ability to cope dropped.

Someone once described fear with this acronym: False Evidence Appearing Real. When we are afraid, we automatically draw the worst conclusions about what is going to happen. People who struggle with anxiety often complain that they are easily distracted, cannot concentrate, and have trouble with their memories. Our thinking automatically becomes fuzzy when we are anxious. When we respond out of raw instinct, we can easily draw irrational conclusions about what we see. Fear distorts our perspective, which directly influences our behavior and feelings, immobilizing us against harmless situations.

Anxious Behavior and Our Feelings

Responses to fear-producing situations can become grossly exaggerated. We chuckle when we remember Nancy, after discovering an infestation of bugs in our house, pummeling a centipede to death in our bathtub with a sledgehammer. The tub remained intact, but the centipede didn't.

When our reaction becomes blown out of proportion, we can become incapacitated by our fear. We end up shadowboxing against what isn't real, draining us of all of our energies.

In addition, what we perceive as threatening leads to anxious behavior and feelings. When mildly threatened, like when we look at our gas gauge and see it is on empty, we may feel some degree of alarm. But if we see the needle at empty as an imminent threat, when we roll to a stop in the middle lane of traffic at rush hour, we may fear the car will stall. We begin to think, *Here I am, a sitting duck for everyone's road rage.* Now much more may happen inside us: Our heart will pound; we break out into a cold sweat; our stomach twists into knots—all because of the heightened perceived threat.

Knowing and Facing Our Fears

Rather than running away and avoiding our fears, we need to identify them and understand how they affect our lives. Tony Campolo retells the story of a laid-off business executive. Overcome with depression, he took a long walk in a park and wondered what he would tell his family that night. He found a bench and sat down to bemoan his situation. At this point, the story takes an unusual turn. The executive has company.

> Another man, equally depressed, came along and sat at the other end of the same bench. He looked over and saw the corporate executive with his head in his hands moaning and groaning to himself and he could not help but ask, "What's wrong with you?"
>
> The executive said, "I've lost my job. I can't go home and tell my family what's happened. They depend on me, and I won't be able to be the good provider I've always been. What's your problem?"
>
> The second man said, "I run a circus and the main attraction has been a huge and threatening gorilla. People came from

all over to watch that gorilla rant and rage at them. Two days ago the gorilla died, and I know my circus won't be able to survive the loss."

"Hey," said the corporate executive. "You need a gorilla and I need employment. I've got an idea. Why don't we skin the gorilla, dress me up in its skin and let me take a try at pretending. We've got nothing to lose. Why not take a chance?"

The agreement was made and the deed was done. In the days that followed, the corporate executive dressed in the gorilla's skin and raged more than the real gorilla ever had. His antics were such that the crowds coming to the circus grew larger and larger, and both men were making a fortune.

Then one day, by sheer accident, a lion ended up in the same cage with the phony gorilla. The crowds gathered to see this incredible confrontation. The lion and the gorilla circled each other as people waited to see what would happen.

Finally, the gorilla realized he was cornered and that there was no escape, and he yelled at the top of his lungs, "HELP!"

The lion shouted back, "Shut up! You're not the only one out of a job!"[6]

Just like the man in the gorilla suit, our fears will be exposed. He thought his life was over until he discovered the lion was just another man out of work. We need to understand and learn about our fears so we can move beyond them.

We all have our own unique fears. Popular author Dave Barry writes, "All of us are born with a set of instinctive fears: of falling, of the dark, of lobsters, of falling on lobsters in the dark, of speaking before a Rotary Club, and of the words: 'some assembly required.'" For some, the words *spider, snake, rat,* or *bridge* may stir within us the urge to scream at the top of our lungs and run for the hills or become frozen dead in our tracks.

Comedian Jerry Seinfeld talks about our major fears when

he wryly states, "I read a thing that speaking in front of a crowd was the number one fear of the average person. I found that amazing. The number two was death. That means for the average person if you have to be at a funeral you would rather be in the casket than delivering the eulogy."[7]

Surprisingly, some notable people in history experienced paralyzing fears:

- Napoleon Bonaparte was known as a great, but he couldn't conquer his obsession to stop in front of tall buildings and count the windows one by one. Napoleon's behavior was an attempt to quell undue anxiety.

- Edgar Allen Poe . . . used his real-life fear of closed spaces to write classic tales as "The Premature Burial" and "The Black Cat."

- Frederick the Great, King of Prussia, was so afraid of water that he wouldn't wash, and instead forced his servants to wipe his face clean with a dry towel.

- John Madden, a six foot, four inch, 240 pound former football player and head coach of the Oakland Raiders professional football team and, today, a well-known TV sports personality, [fears jet travel. Instead of flying,] he travels the country in his specially equipped luxury bus, donated for his use by Greyhound.[8]

Each of these leaders evidenced his fear and anxiety by developing a specific phobia. Anxiety is a general feeling of fearfulness devoid of a specific object where a phobia is a specific fear. A phobia is an irrational fear of something that is not dangerous or a perception of something dangerous that is blown out of proportion to the actual danger. The reactions of someone who has a phobia can range from a moderate degree of anxiety to high levels of panic. The physical symptoms are similar to general anxiety: difficulty in breathing, sweating, heart palpitations, etc.

People who have phobias will try to avoid at all cost the object or situation they are afraid of. They eliminate things they would normally do to find temporary relief from an anxiety-producing situation. Yet avoidance of the situation only perpetuates the problem.

Phobias can develop for practically anything. Common phobias are the fear of snakes, spiders, and speaking in public, formally known as herpetophobia, arachnophobia, and glossophobia, respectively. Other common phobias include the fear of heights (acrophobia), enclosed spaces (claustrophobia), open spaces (agoraphobia), and even the bogeyman (bogyphobia). Each of these fears can become our Achilles' heel and render us emotionally disabled.

We have seen in this chapter the various physical, cognitive, and emotional aspects of fear. How we perceive situations, how our body responds, and what specifically we fear all are intertwined together. Although the things people fear are endless, in this book we are addressing fears that directly affect connections with others. Four specific fears are: the fear of failure, fear of rejection, fear of abandonment, and fear of dying (both emotionally and physically).

These fears can debilitate any relationship. Any one of them can undermine the yearning we have to connect deeply with others, effectively blocking our ability to maintain healthy, loving relationships. The good news is every one of us can learn to become fear managers by learning what specific relational fears are blocking us. Once we recognize those fears, we can reconnect with others and acquire the skills to love more deeply.

The Battle for Love in Relationships

*Only when we are no longer afraid
do we begin to live. . . .*

·❖·

DOROTHY THOMPSON

J ust as it is a mystery to explain the transformation of a cater-pillar into a butterfly, it is difficult to express the mystery of how we can recover from the years of hurt and bitterness that have developed our fears. All we can do is watch with wonder the transformation of people who choose to replace their fear with love.

This transformation can occur only when we apply certain guidelines of life to our interactions with our loved ones. Just as the butterfly's struggle to come out of the cocoon is an important part of the butterfly's development, so it is with personal growth. As we each struggle through the hard work and diligence of growth, we find the result to be a newfound freedom to love without the bondage of fear.

Fear unchecked has a devastating effect on our ability to love and be loved. When driven by fear, we are likely to do destructive things to the people we love and to ourselves. We can become so fearful we harm others out of a misplaced impulse to protect ourselves. Phil Yancey clarifies, "The opposite of fear is not courage, but love. Unconditional love is a powerful antidote to the toxin of unhealthy fear."[1] To realize this, we must be willing to choose to conquer our fears. In this chapter we will describe what makes up a loving relationship and what blocks us. We will learn how we come to know love, how we can be hurt in loving relationships when someone we love becomes afraid and, most importantly, how love can be restored by finding healing from our hurts.

Our Deepest Longing

An ancient Irish phrase states, "Anyone without a soul-friend is like a body without a head." This saying speaks of our instinctual desire for close and meaningful relationships. As early as the seventh century, the church of Ireland advised people to develop a soul-friend relationship with someone who would be trusted for a lifetime as a confidante and spiritual guide. The church described a soul-friend relationship as one where there was a profound sense of trust, in which people could confess their darkest secrets and receive counsel.

Our need to be understood in a loving and nurturing relationship with another is no different today than it was fourteen hundred years ago. We want the type of relationships that motivate us to grow and become people we could have never imagined. In spite of all of the healing and hope relationships can give us, we struggle with taking the leap to give and receive love. Yet it still is our deepest longing. We all desire relationships that are rich, satisfying, and caring. When we are truly loved, we are liberated to become all of who our Creator desires us to be;

we find security as well as freedom.

We all long to feel safe with someone. In every relationship, we long for someone with whom we feel so safe that we are willing to take risks. On their fiftieth anniversary, Bob and Charlotte Ann O'Donnell told friends gathered for the occasion about that risk-taking love, first shown during Bob's courtship. They laughed when they recalled those early days as young lovers filled with dreams to last a lifetime.

"When love hit," remembered Bob, recalling when they first met, "we were hit hard!"

"I remember one night, soon after Bob proposed," Charlotte Ann noted, "telling him that I just couldn't marry him if he didn't have any money."

"I saw this as a challenge," Bob replied.

"The next thing I knew," Charlotte Ann continued, "he was back at my house with a bank book in his hand with $300.00 in the balance.

"Needless to say, I was amazed and thrilled and said to Bob that we should go out to eat and celebrate! I got my coat and we headed out the door; only to my surprise Bob's car was nowhere to be found. Puzzled, I turned to Bob. Like a boy with his hand stuck in a cookie jar, he sheepishly admitted, 'I sold the car so we could get married.'

"And that," Charlotte Ann concluded, "is the way our life has been ever since!"[2]

Bob's love for Charlotte Ann is an example of the risks—and sacrifices—we are willing to make for those we love.

Viktor Frankl survived Nazi concentration camps in Bohemia and Auschwitz but lost his wife in the Holocaust (he later remarried). He wrote the classic *Man's Search for Meaning* and concluded (as Bob and Charlotte Ann would discover during their first fifty years together): "The truth [is] that love is the ultimate and the highest goal to which man can aspire."

A Love That Puts Life in Perspective

When someone loves us, we find healing, meaning to life, and a reason for living. When someone loves us, we are able to put the disappointments of life in perspective. Harold Kushner, author of *When Bad Things Happen to Good People,* observed this principle in action one summer day while sitting on the beach, watching a boy and a girl forming a sandcastle.

They were hard at work, by the water's edge, building an elaborate sandcastle with gates and towers and moats and internal passages.

Just when they had nearly finished their project, a big wave came along and knocked it down, reducing it to a heap of wet sand. I expected the children to burst into tears, devastated by what had happened to all their work. But they surprised me, they ran up the shore away from the water, laughing and holding hands, and sat down to build another castle.

I realized that they had taught me an important lesson. All the things in our lives, all the complicated structures we spend so much time and energy creating, are built on sand. Only our relationships to other people endure. Sooner or later, the wave will come along and knock down what we have worked so hard to build up. When that happens, only the person who has somebody's hand to hold will be able to laugh.[3]

The love we experience in relationships is a faint echo of God's love for us. "We love because he first loved us," the apostle John wrote (1 John 4:19). He is the source of all love. God loves us perfectly and unconditionally and shows us what true love is. Yet somewhere between our desires and the divine ideal we all have experienced deep wounds of disappointment and betrayal.

Loving and Taking Risks

C.S. Lewis said it well. "To love at all is to be vulnerable. Love anything, and your heart will certainly be wrung and possibly broken."[4] To love someone is to open ourselves up to glaring inspection, risking ridicule and rejection. Yet when we risk, what exactly do we gain?

Risk and Gain

Dr. Richard Selzer gives us a glimpse of what we gain in the following story of one of his patients. He describes a poignant interaction he observed between a young man and his wife following facial surgery that left her with a crooked smile.

> I stand by the bed where a young woman lies, her face postoperative, her mouth twisted in palsy, clownish. A tiny twig of the facial nerve, the one to the muscles in her mouth, was severed [when I removed] the tumor in her cheek. Although she is free from the tumor her crooked mouth will always be a reminder of the painful ordeal.
>
> Her young husband is in the room. He stands on the opposite side of the bed, and together they seem to dwell in the evening lamplight, isolated from me, private. Who are they, I ask myself . . . [as they] gaze at each other so generously greedily? The young woman speaks.
>
> "Will my mouth always be like this?" she asks.
>
> "Yes," I say, "it will. It is because the nerve was cut."
>
> She nods and is silent. But the young man smiles.
>
> "I like it," he says. "I think it is kind of cute."

In their intimate moment, the surgeon lowers his gaze and

feels humbled, as in some "encounter with a god." Dr. Selzer describes what happened next:

> Unmindful, he bends to kiss her crooked mouth, and I so close I can see how he twists his own lips to accommodate to hers, to show her that their kiss still works. I remember that the gods appeared in ancient Greece as mortals, and I hold my breath and let the wonder in.[5]

We would disagree with Dr. Selzer; the loving husband is not a god but a man—though one who deeply loves his wife and soul mate. He is willing to accept her completely at a time when she is most vulnerable. And his wife is a woman of remarkable courage—willing to risk being seen and loved at such a vulnerable moment in her life. They give us a glimmer of the strength, comfort, and hope we can find in loving relationships.

Risk and Possible Loss

We can all think of times in which the people we valued and cared for deeply disappointed us by their lack of approval or love. Perhaps we felt it from a parent who constantly reminded us that our value to them was measured by our last report card, or from the painful sting of the harsh words by our former spouse as he/she slammed the front door, never to return. We might have felt disappointment in love when our childhood best friend, who professed lifelong loyalty, soon found new interests and relationships—and spending time with us was not one of them. Or we may have felt it when, as a grown adult, we were with our families and felt their silent blasts of shame and ridicule filled with judgments and jealousies. We realize how deeply we need to be loved when we are deeply injured by those we choose to risk loving.

In his classic book *Unconditional Love,* John Powell wrote,

Going to another in love means risk—the risks of self disclosure, rejection and misunderstanding. It means grief, too, from the temporary separations, psychological or physical, to the final separation of death. Whoever insists on personal security and safety as the nonnegotiable conditions of life will not be willing to pay love's price or find love's enrichments. Whoever shuts himself or herself up in the cocoon of self protective defenses, keeping others always at a safe distance . . . will find the price of love far too high and will remain a prisoner of fear.[6]

In all of these experiences, our natural inclination is to develop a protection from others and build impenetrable walls of defense from the pain.

Pain Deflectors

Every one of us, at one time or another, develops pain deflectors. Just as we wear sunscreen in order to avoid getting sun poisoning, our pain deflectors keep us from being emotionally burned. They are a way we keep ourselves from feeling the hurt of rejection in a relationship. Our pain deflectors might be staying distant from others, refusing to feel deep emotion, or keeping a hectic schedule so we don't have time to think about our real needs.

While the particular deflector may keep us from feeling more pain, it will also keep us from experiencing true and meaningful levels of intimacy.

When we become emotionally frozen by our fears, we are unable to have our significant longings for love realized. When we lock fear in our hearts because we have been hurt, our natural reaction is to bury those hurts and fears alive (rather than let them die). When we make the decision, whether consciously or not, to bury our feelings, the consequence results in our sentencing our heart to a term of solitary confinement—locked up and unable to truly connect and freely love others.

Disabling Fear

"We are afraid of truth, afraid of fortune, afraid of death, and afraid of each other," said American writer and philosopher Ralph Waldo Emerson.[7] During our over forty combined years of working with people, we have consistently found that the most destructive emotion in relationships is fear. Fear disables us; it robs us of the joy that can be found in loving relationships. As Henri Nouwen noted:

> The more people I come to know and the more I come to know people, the more I am overwhelmed by the negative power of fear. It often seems that fear has invaded every part of our being to such a degree that we no longer know what a life without fear would feel like. . . . In many, often-subtle ways fear victimizes and controls us. Fear can make us upset and angry. It can drive us into depression or despair. It can surround us with darkness and make us feel close to destruction and death.[8]

When we become afraid, we rob ourselves of the ability to love. We then avoid being close to those we care most about. Motivated by the need for safety, we distance ourselves emotionally, and at times physically, to protect ourselves from the threat of being hurt. "Fear is the great enemy of intimacy," Nouwen declared. "Fear makes us run away from each other or cling to each other but does not create true intimacy."[9]

Jordan grew up in severe poverty. His father was a migrant

worker in the fields of California. When he came to my (Ray's) office for counseling, Jordan recalled his childhood as a constant movement from one area to another with barely enough to eat. He had a loving family, but the strain of poverty took its toll on everyone.

Jordan remembered sitting behind an old elm tree one day as a young boy and overhearing two of the crop managers in the field talking about his dad. "John is a nice guy, but he will never amount to anything."

Jordan felt his heart sink, and his face become hot with the flush of embarrassment and shame. He also felt angry with those men for what they said and afraid of what would happen to his dad and the family.

"I can remember deciding that day," Jordan told me, "that I would never be embarrassed like that again, and I would be a good provider for my family."

Jordan's fear of becoming a failure, as the men perceived his dad to be, drove him as an adult to become a high-level executive. He was determined to succeed at any cost. Unwilling and unable to slow down, he never really noticed that he was moving toward emotional brokenness and failure in his relationships.

For Jordan, the long hours at work were the price he had to pay for controlling his fears. His relationship with his wife was cordial but lacked warmth and closeness. Relationships were few because they took too much energy away from his daily work activities. Understanding his own emotional needs was a risk he was unwilling to take. When his wife said she needed more time with him, he would lash out in uncontrolled anger, afraid that what he perceived as his wife's demands would somehow threaten his chances of becoming a success.

Sadly, Jordan's marriage ended in a painful divorce. He became a financial success, but disappointment and failure marked his personal relationships. Disabling fear destroyed his relationship with his wife.

"All human failures are the result of lack of love," psychologist Alfred Adler has said. Jordan's decision to avoid pain and refusal to face his fear of ridicule drove him to workaholism and created greater pain for him in his present circumstance; in his determination to manage his fears he lost the tender love of his wife along the way.

Fear of Pain

"One of the most common obstacles to celebrating life fully is our avoidance of pain," wrote Clyde Reid, an associate professor at the University of Denver's School of Theology. "We dread pain. We fear pain. We do anything to escape pain. Our culture reinforces our avoidance of pain by assuring us that we can live a painless life."[10]

In his book *Celebrate the Temporary,* Reid describes the myth of such a life:

> Advertisements constantly encourage us to believe that life can be pain-free [but] to live without pain is a myth. . . . To live without pain . . . is to live half-alive, without fullness of life. This is an unmistakable, clear unalterable fact. . . . Many of us do not realize that pain and joy run together. When we cut ourselves off from pain, we have unwittingly cut ourselves off from joy as well."[11]

All of us, to varying degrees, have had painful events locked in our hearts and minds. We react to these experiences with fear that they will happen again. When these fears are not dealt with, they can quickly lead to what is called "catastrophic thinking." When we think catastrophically, we set into motion, like dominoes falling, a process of thinking that causes us to draw conclusions that the worst possible outcomes are going to occur—that somehow we will be the recipient of our most dreaded fears.

We can remember when our son, Eric, came back from his karate class and with great enthusiasm began to show Ray his new moves. Without warning he jumped on Ray's back, put him into a headlock, and said, "Where the head goes, the body goes!"

Ray was startled but Eric was right. Similarly, when we have locked fear in our souls, over time our thinking becomes driven by our anxiety and controls our reactions and behaviors. We can draw irrational conclusions like, "If I ever open my heart again I'll never survive," or "Trust only yourself," or "The pain of being rejected is too much to risk," or "Good fences make good neighbors."

The Choice

We have a choice as to how we will deal with the pain we have felt in relationships. We can choose to be controlled by our fears, or we can choose to let them be a catalyst for healing and change.

"God has given us two incredible things: absolutely awesome ability and freedom of choice. The tragedy is that, for the most part, many of us have refused them both," says Frank Donnelly.[12] We can decide to look at our pain, to look at the root source of our fear, and to look at how it has affected our relationships. We can decide either to transform them into crucibles of joy, or we can become angry, bitter, and emotionally paralyzed.

There is an old and well-known story that vividly illustrates the power of choices.

There were once two men, both seriously ill, in the same small room of a great hospital. [It was] a small room, just large enough for the pair of them—two beds, two bedside lockers, and a door opening on the hall and one window looking out on the world.

One of the men, as part of his treatment, was allowed to sit up in bed for an hour in the afternoon next to the window (something to do with draining the fluid from his lungs), and his bed was next to the window.

But the other man had to spend all his time flat on his back. . . . Both of them had to remain quiet and still, which was the reason they were in the small room by themselves. . . . They were grateful for peace and privacy—none of the hustle and bustle and prying eyes of the general ward for them.

Of course, one of the disadvantages of their condition was that they weren't allowed to do much: no reading, no radio, certainly no television—just had to keep still, just the two of them.

Well, they used to talk for hours and hours—about their wives, their children, their homes, their jobs, their hobbies, their childhood, what they did during the war, where they'd been on vacations—all that sort of thing.

Every afternoon, when the man in the bed next to the window was propped up for his hour, he would pass the time by describing what he could see outside. And the other man began to live for those hours.

The window apparently overlooked a park, with a lake, where there were ducks and swans, children throwing them bread and sailing model boats, and young lovers walking hand in hand beneath the trees. . . . There were flowers and stretches of grass . . . games of softball, people [laying] in the sun, and right at the back, behind the fringe of trees, a fine view of the city skyline.

The man on his back would listen to all of this, enjoying every minute—how a child nearly fell into the lake, how beautiful the girls were in their summer dresses, then an exciting ball game, or a boy playing with his puppy. It got to the place that he could almost *see* what was happening outside.

Then one fine afternoon, when [he heard outside] some sort of parade, the thought struck him. Why should the man next to the window have all the pleasure of seeing what was going on? Why shouldn't he get the chance?

He felt ashamed and tried not to think like that, but the more he tried the worse he wanted a change. He'd do anything!

In a few days, he had turned sour. He should be by the window. And he brooded, and couldn't sleep, and grew even more seriously ill—which none of the doctors understood.

One night as he stared at the ceiling, the other man suddenly woke up, coughing and choking, the fluid congesting in his lungs, his hands groping for the button that would bring the night nurse running. But the man watched without moving.

The coughing racked the darkness—on and on . . . then stopped—the sound of breathing stopped—and the man continued to stare at the ceiling.

In the morning the day nurse came in with water for their baths and found the other man dead. They took away his body, quietly, no fuss.

As soon as it seemed decent, the man asked if he could be moved to the bed next to the window. And they moved him, tucked him in, and made him quite comfortable, and left him alone to be quiet and still.

The minute they'd gone, anxious to finally get his chance, the man painfully and laboriously propped himself up on one elbow, and looked out the window.

It faced a blank wall.[13]

There are those of us who spend our entire lives blaming others, emotionally locked up in fear, trying desperately to control others and secretly envying those around us. There are also those of us who face fears and pain as seemingly insurmountable as this one man's "blank wall," yet see them as opportunities to grow and to bring life and beauty to those we know.

The story of these two men touches a chord in our souls. It shows us that when we choose to control others and circumstances out of our fear and pain, we miss the chance to see the free gifts of love that people give us. If we don't come to grips with our fear, then, like the man who longed to sit at the window, we will have gained what we thought we wanted only to find that we have lost love in the process.

Love Restored

Can we ever salvage a relationship after a season of constant battling, hurt, and fear where love was denied and the risk seemed too great? George and Heather asked the same question, and then they came to Ray for counseling.

After they arrived, it soon became clear they were only steps away from the courthouse. Emotionally beaten by the years of constant conflict, their marriage of thirty-four years was crumbling before their eyes. George had moved out of the house, but he was willing to come in for marriage counseling as a last-ditch effort.

Over time the emotional distance they had created in their marriage seemed as wide as the Grand Canyon. They were married but living single lives. Their hurts had turned to aching bitterness.

George felt that Heather was controlling and needed to have things done her way. He felt he could never get close to her. Heather would say George neither wanted to listen or take personal responsibility for their financial difficulties. She felt he was preoccupied and uncaring.

Both George and Heather had built walls that effectively kept them from having to deal with the fear of getting close. Heather protected herself by "being in charge." From home decor to the discipline of their children, as long as Heather felt in control she felt she wasn't at risk of being hurt by George. George protected himself by being absorbed in his own world and found his safety in being emotionally unavailable.

Fortunately, George and Heather became willing to face their disappointments and hurts. As they did, this couple was able to identify the powerful fears that had been motivating them. They learned that each feared closeness and had developed patterns to avoid being hurt. Ironically, those patterns became the very source of the pain in their relationship.

As they faced these fears head-on, they were able to defuse the power the fears had on them. Heather recognized that her need for control pushed George away. As she let go of her need to be in charge, she found George feeling more relaxed and open with her. George, on the other hand, identified his fear of being an adequate provider in their marriage. As he explored the reasons behind these fears, he was able to establish a budget and a proactive plan for them to move out of their financial difficulties. It was the open and honest sharing of their fears that was pivotal in their relationship being restored.

Later George said to Ray, "If I wouldn't have addressed these issues in our marriage, I believe I would have lived the rest of my years as a lonely, bitter man. I am so thankful for Heather and the love we now have."

What Our Fears Reveal

We wrongfully conclude along the way that to have fear means we are cowards and weak-willed people. Instead, our fears reveal how we have been hurt and show the tender places in our hearts. No matter how insignificant and silly our fears may seem to us, they reveal to others where we most need understanding and care.

To honestly recognize and express our fears to someone requires profound trust. It is saying to the other person, "Because I know you love me, I am willing to take a risk and show you where I am most vulnerable." Daphne Rose Kingma writes in *The Book of Love:*

> Interestingly enough, revealing what you are afraid of usually prompts the other person to divulge his or her fears too. In this way, exposing your fears puts you at once in alignment with the innermost self of the other person, with what he's afraid of, with where she feels terrified and alone. So reveal your fears, because it is being together in the midst of our vulnerabilities that is one of the most tender and touching experiences of being in love.[14]

As they risked sharing their deepest fears with each other, George and Heather realized a depth of intimacy in their relationship that they had not previously experienced. After courageous sharing, forgiving each other, and healing, George and Heather came to a place where they wanted to renew their wedding vows. Their relationship had changed so significantly they felt they wanted to make a symbolic new beginning. Today, they are now realizing all the joys and benefits a healthy marriage provides; they are supporting each other, listening to each other, sharing their feelings with each other in ways they never dreamed possible.

We *can* find restoration in our relationships, but it requires each of us to look carefully at how fear has become a wedge in our relating to others. In the next chapter, we will look closely at four specific relational fears—failure, rejection, abandonment, and death—and see how they paralyze us from risking and loving others. When we face our fears, we gain greater freedom in our lives to truly celebrate the relationships we have been given.

The Major Relational Fears

It is not death that a man should fear, but he should fear never beginning to live.

⁜

MARCUS AURELIUS

The famous psychiatrist Karl Menninger was asked what was the single most significant aspect of helping others. Was it being compassionate? Was it being an effective listener? Was it quality training? He replied with one word: *diagnosis.*

We cannot help someone until we have diagnosed what the problem actually is, he explained. We can be the most compassionate people in the world, but until we have determined the core problem we cannot help anyone.

In the same way, we will find freedom from fear when we recognize the specific type(s) of fear inhibiting us from enjoying our relationships. In this chapter we will explain four major fears that affect relationships. Each section begins with a person (actually a composite of people we've met) who typifies the fear in action and concludes with a symptom checklist to help determine if the particular fear is afflicting our lives.

The Fear of Failure

Georgia is a woman who appears to have it all. She has a loving husband, three beautiful grade-school children, and a prestigious position as an account executive for a well-known advertising agency. She has been targeted as the next person to fill a senior management position. However, the demands of her job require her to work ten-hour days. While she is excited about the opportunities in front of her, she feels guilty leaving her children with a sitter every day.

Georgia can't seem to pull herself away from her work. She fears if she pulls back her career will suffer and confirm her worst fear—that she is deeply incompetent. She seems to be able to manage the demands of her children, home, and marriage; but at the end of the day she is emotionally and physically exhausted. Georgia wonders how long she will be able to keep up the pace.

When Georgia's husband brings up the topic of how much time she spends at work, she responds defensively by stating that if she cuts back, the family will lose the comfortable lifestyle they have both worked hard to achieve. In spite of her accomplishments, Georgia feels a deep sense of anxiety that she is only one step away from failure. She struggles over her roles as a mother, wife, and career person. Somehow, Georgia reasons, if she just keeps pushing hard, she feels she can avoid failing in any of her roles. Georgia's fear of failure is destroying her.

Trying to Meet Expectations

The fear of failure says, "I am only as good as my last performance. I need to keep pushing hard to ensure success because if I don't I will fail." As adults we have expectations from friends, spouses, family, coworkers, and bosses dictating the way we act or behave. Our culture measures us based on our actions. The football player is judged by the number of touchdowns he gets or passes he catches. An employee's job performance is measured by how well she has acted on the directions given by her supervisor. As children we are rewarded with an ice cream cone if we behaved well at Aunt Betty's. When we experience fear of failure, it is as if we perceive we are under a magnifying glass. We feel every move is dissected and judged.

The fear of failure can make us feel as though our entire competency as a person is on the line. It is like going into a room with voting ballots in hand, giving everyone a ballot and asking them to vote on our performance. We define ourselves by our capabilities rather than our worth and value. The fear of failure can become so emotionally absorbing that it depletes us from having any energy to connect with those we love.

Some of us become so overwhelmed by this fear we do not even try anything new in our lives. We conclude, "Why take the risk when there is so much to lose?" We become besieged with a sense of panic when we are not meeting our expectations or what we perceive are the expectations of others. Like a deer frozen in the road, staring in fear at the oncoming headlights, we stop dead in our tracks. We discontinue a task or fail to initiate a task we had planned to do if we see there is risk involved. We look for diversions so that we don't have to think about our anxious feelings and try to silence the negative thoughts inside.

Looking at Success as "Good Luck"

Others of us may take risks in new situations and in fact succeed, but we interpret our victory not as a measure of our capabilities but as a stroke of good luck. Consequently, when we are commended for our success, we minimize and discount the sincerity of the compliments we receive. When Bob Fosse, one of Broadway's brilliant choreographers in the '60s and '70s, received an Oscar, a Tony, and an Emmy all in one year, he told his friends, "I fooled everybody." His response is common for those of us dealing with this particular fear. When success occurs for us, we are unwilling to take ownership for it.

Deep within us, when we struggle with this fear, we feel somehow defective. To compensate, we counterbalance our fear of failure by setting high and unrealistic expectations. These expectations are often expressed through perfectionistic tendencies.

"Underneath overblown pride, or narcissism, is the opposite feeling—that you are inherently flawed," Sharon Heller explains. In her book *The Complete Idiot's Guide to Conquering Fear and Anxiety,* she says people strive for perfection to compensate; they also set unrealistically high expectations for themselves and others. And when they don't succeed?

> When, inevitably, things fall short, you become disappointed and self-critical. Even when enormously successful, you zoom in on the fly in the ointment and tend to discount and ignore what's good. You compare yourself to others, minimize your own achievements and feel like a failure—worse than nothing. And you project this self hate onto others and assume that they too despise you for being so defective.[1]

When we feel the fear of failure, we block ourselves from moving forward and celebrating our abilities, achievements, and blessings.

Signs of the Fear of Failure

In summary, the telltale signs of the fear of failure include:

- Viewing our worth by our abilities.
- Avoiding situations that involve learning new skills and abilities.
- Becoming paralyzed when thinking of taking a risk or striving beyond what is necessary to ensure success.
- Degrading our achievements and ourselves.
- Valuing others' measure of us more than our own.
- Playing negative messages in our head such as, "I will never be good enough," "I have failed at everything I have tried," "I am not talented enough," and "I'll never make it, so why bother?"
- Comparing ourselves to others and perceiving them as more successful, competent, talented, etc.
- Having the need for things in which we are involved to be perfect, such as being the perfect decorator, perfect friend, perfect parent, or perfect coworker.
- Confusing our performance with love.
- Never really being at peace.

Fear of Rejection

Everyone loved Laura. She was the type of person that never said a cross word or had a bad day. Even in the midst of the demands of raising five children, her sunny disposition seemed to lift the spirits of whoever she was around.

Laura was always eager to please others. She was the first person the grade school would call when they needed a parent to supervise the playground. When she was asked by the church to help out with their weekly children's program she agreed. She was the leader for her daughter's Girl Scouts because there were no other parents who would volunteer, and she didn't want to disappoint her daughter. Laura found it difficult to say no when asked to head up the fund-raiser for the eighth-grade class trip because she didn't want her son's teacher to see her as an unsupportive parent.

In fact, Laura's life was overrun by activities because she couldn't say no. She confided in a friend that she was secretly angry that so many people had expectations of her but feared saying no because she didn't want them to think less of her. One time Laura said no to a request to help set up a class party. When word got back that the teacher was disappointed and missed her, Laura felt horrible that her daughter's teacher would think poorly of her. She called and apologized, but she couldn't shake the anxious feeling that the teacher saw her differently now. Laura was driven by a fear of rejection.

Hearts That Sink

The experiences of rejection in our lives can cause our hearts to sink, our heads to drop, and an inner voice to say, "I am not OK." When we sense personal rejection, it often feels like an earthquake that measures 7.9 on the Richter scale. The rejection rocks our soul and causes the bricks of our self-worth to fall. To be rejected means that who we are is not of value to others.

This sinking heart was represented by a patient at the Adult Anxiety Clinic at Temple University being counseled by the clinic's Richard Heimberg. As Heimberg recently told *Time* magazine,

> the 50-year-old patient . . . talked frequently about getting married and having a family—a reasonable dream, except that his terror of rejection had kept him from ever going out on a date.

After much encouragement and counseling, he finally summoned up enough courage to ask a woman out. The next day, when Heimberg asked him if he'd had a good time, he said yes. However, when asked if he were going to invite her out again, the patient slumped and said no. "She's only going to give to charity once," he explained.[2]

Most of us first experienced some form of rejection in childhood. In families where there were high expectations of achievement or there was a personality conflict between a parent and child, there was a heightened sensitivity to rejection.

Sheldon Kopp, a psychologist, explains how the seeds of rejection are sown in our souls.

If our parents treated us as worthy of respect in our own right, then by the time we grew up, we felt at ease in revealing ourselves and expected that some people would be pleased to know who we were. But if we had parents who were unaccepting of our independent identities, we learned to hide who we really were for fear that we were not allowed to be ourselves. We created the illusion that all we wanted was to fulfill our parents' needs. In the safety of isolation from parental intrusions, we sustained a secret self. We coped with childhood fears by hiding what we really felt, and grew up afraid that unless we met other people's expectations, they would reject us."[3]

Masks That Cover Our Hearts

When we experience rejection over time, we develop "masks" that cover our true selves and protect our hearts from hurt and shame. When we put on the masks, like actors on the stage, we perform in ways we perceive others want from us. Virginia Satir, a noted family therapist, refers to this dynamic as placating behavior. It is as if we are posturing ourselves before others on bended knee, emotionally pleading for their approval. We are hoping, by pleasing them, we can minimize painful criticism and judgments. Our need is to somehow secure love and acceptance through "right" behavior. The irony of it is that even when we are affirmed we are not willing to believe it, because behind our mask of performance we feel we are unworthy.

We can wear a variety of masks. For example, some of us may wear the mask of the "good person" or pleaser. When we wear this mask, we are always making sure that others like us, even if that means we compromise our own values and opinions. Others of us may put on the mask of a clown. Wearing the clown mask means we spend our lives entertaining others and making sure they are happy even when we are not being true to our real emotions and needs. And some of us may wear the mask of the philosopher. Wearing this mask means we remain detached from the real world of feelings, presenting the image that nothing really affects us. The philosopher is always above the world, making judgments and never really letting others in.

The fear of rejection has such a powerful influence that we allow others to control our very lives. Peter G. Van Breeman expands on this idea. "This fear of ridicule paralyzes more effectively than would a head-on attack or an outspoken harsh criticism. How much good is left undone because of our fear of the opinion of others! The irony of all this is that the opinions we fear most are not those of people we really respect, yet these same persons' opinions carry more weight than we are willing to admit. This enervating fear of our peers can create an appalling mediocrity."[4]

Keeping Our Distance

Another aspect of the fear of rejection is avoiding deep relationships, remaining distant and aloof, and concluding that it is better not to be involved than to be hurt.

No one would have thought Dan was like that. After all, he was the life of the party; his playfulness and engaging humor charmed everyone. He was a natural in his job as a sales rep for a large pharmaceutical company. From a distance it appeared he had a charmed life—a beautiful wife, good kids, nice home, and successful career. Everyone who talked with Dan assumed he enjoyed people, but, in truth, people only knew him on a shallow level.

Beyond the facade was a different man—in fact, there were two Dans. The one Dan was successful, optimistic, and everyone's friend. The other Dan was lonely, self-absorbed, and continually anxious. He was dreadfully afraid of what others thought of him. He was hypervigilant in trying to please others.

Dan had not only become an expert at sizing up what people wanted but also became an expert at delivering it. If he was with his golf buddies, he knew the latest scores of all the top professional golfers. If he was with his wife's family, he made sure he was seen as a sensitive and thoughtful husband and father. If he was at work, he was the tough competitor.

Inside, though, he felt weak, inadequate, scared, and tired. Lonely and unsure of himself, Dan was weary of keeping the game going. He wanted to be himself.

Dan had become a prisoner of his own self-imposed cell. Every conversation he had was an internal battle to silence the condemning doubts and insecurities. He felt second-rate to everyone he met and longed to be set free from his self-imposed bondage. His pattern had become so established that it seemed impossible for him to behave any other way. He ached for relationships in which he could be vulnerable, accepted, and loved. He felt the bond that he had with his wife was based on the responsibilities they each fulfilled rather than an intimate sharing of life's joys and sorrows together. His fear of rejection profoundly affected his relationship with his wife and everyone he longed to be close to.

Signs of the Fear of Rejection

The fear of rejection ties us up from being free to be who we were created to be. The signs of the fear of rejection include:

- Trying to read people's minds and assuming they will not like us.
- Being distrustful of others and anticipating that we will be harmed.
- Developing a self-perception that if someone got to know the real us, that person wouldn't really like us.
- Allowing others to dictate how we feel about our lives and ourselves.
- Constantly trying to please others.
- Second-guessing our reactions and decisions.

The Fear of Abandonment

We knew Nathan as an adult, but his greatest fear began as a child.[5] Nathan grew up in a home in which he was the one boy among five older sisters. His mother had been through two painful divorces by the time Nathan was six. She had developed a deep resentment and bitterness toward men. The pressure of raising the children alone became too much for her. Nathan became a constant reminder of her simmering anger toward men.

"I can recall it like it was yesterday, although I was a young kid at the time," Nathan told us. "My mom got me all dressed up, and I didn't know why. The next thing I knew, she put me in a cab and gave the cab driver money. She sent me to live with some relatives that I had never met.

"I remember screaming and crying and trying to get out of the cab. I looked out from the cab window as it pulled away from the curb. There I saw my sisters crying too and waving good-bye." Nathan cried all the way to his relatives' house and felt fully rejected by his mother. He could not understand why his mom felt the need to get rid of him and continue to raise his sisters.

Nancy recalls Nathan saying that as a young child he was determined that he would survive. For most of his life he fought against an alarming feeling that there was something terribly wrong with him and that if someone really got to know him he or she would leave.

Nathan's life was haunted by the fear of abandonment, a fear that affects its sufferers more profoundly than the fear of rejection. If rejection is like an earthquake registering 7.9 on the Richter scale, then the fear of abandonment is like a twenty-megaton bomb going off in our souls. To be abandoned is the demoralizing experience of being given up on, left alone and deserted. One feels forsaken.

Feeling Empty . . . Suspicious

The experiences of abandonment leave us cracked, chipped, and broken relationally. We feel empty inside and long to have this void filled. We are forever looking to find someone who might fill up the barrenness we feel inside.

Abandonment, whether it is physical or emotional, leaves us suspicious that others in our life will leave too. That's how Nathan felt. He became timid and had an unquenchable thirst for love and acceptance. Yet he, like all who feel abandoned, always sus-pected the loyalty and security of those who said they loved him.

To use another image, an abandoned person is like a prize horse that is neglected. A beautiful quarter horse enters the world with the potential to one day run like the wind, muscles rippling, able to outrace almost every other kind of horse. If this horse is well taken care of—fed well, exercised, and groomed —it will fulfill its full destiny. But suppose the owner neglects the horse: It will become malnourished and disease ridden, lose the ability to run, and never develop to its full potential. Like that neglected quarter horse, when we have been abandoned, we lose the ability to become all of who God created us to be.

Emotional Hibernation

When we have been abandoned, we go into a form of emotional hibernation. We keep ourselves emotionally removed in order to deaden the painful experiences of our earlier losses in an attempt to reduce the pain of ever being abandoned again.

In the fear of abandonment, we actually give up our sense of ourselves to guarantee a relationship. It is like selling our car for food when we are starving. Our hunger is immediately satisfied, but we have lost the ability to feed ourselves for the following days.

Counselor and inspirational speaker John Bradshaw notes that many children experience abandonment in several ways, including the following:

- By their parents physically leaving.
- By their parents not modeling their own emotions for the children.
- By their parents not providing for the children's developmental dependency needs.

- By their parents physically, sexually, emotionally, and spiritually abusing them.

- By their parents using them to take care of the parents' own unmet dependency needs.

- By their parents using them in order to take care of the parents' marriages.

- By their parents not giving them time, attention, and direction.

- By their parents acting shameless.[6]

Bradshaw explains, "In abandonment the order of nature is reversed. Children have to take care of their parents. There is no one to take care of them. The preciousness and uniqueness, which every human child possesses, is destroyed through abandonment. The child is alone and alienated."[7]

Signs of the Fear of Abandonment

Those of us who have felt abandoned will show many of the following behaviors in our lives:

- Developing a sense of insecurity where we want to attach ourselves to other people for strength and support yet remain emotionally aloof.

- Having difficulty in trusting others.

- Questioning what healthy love is because the love we first experienced was conditional.

- Denying our own needs and feelings in order to secure love from others.

- Developing a rescue personality where we seek out needy people who are unwilling to take responsibility for their own pain.
- Seeking out relationships with people who are unreliable and will ultimately abandon us.

Fear of Death

Most of us think of fear of death in terms of the grave. Certainly physical death is a major fear, especially as we age. Yet there is another fear we encounter in life: the fear of emotional death. It is to this fear we turn next.

Fear of Dying Emotionally

Derek, one of the golden boys of the commodities market, was confident and brash. Then one month in the late '80s, the financial markets took a nosedive, and Derek's high-risk investments dove as well, spiraling his company toward bankruptcy. The company that he had spent years building was about to go under. To complicate matters, he discovered soon after that his partner had embezzled a significant amount of money. He sought financial help from his friends in the business only to be abruptly turned down.

The ongoing strain of these circumstances took its toll on his marriage and children. His wife of fifteen years announced one morning that she had had enough and wanted a divorce.

At the end of another twelve-hour day, frantically trying to pull his circumstances together, Derek checked himself into the emergency room. He was having trouble breathing and was shaking uncontrollably. He thought he was having a heart attack; or worse, that he was losing his mind. The doctors, however, found nothing.

Derek felt so down by his circumstances he thought his very life was being choked out. He feared for his very survival and wondered how he could ever go on.

An Overload That Overwhelms

Derek was clearly overwhelmed by his crumbling world. Few of us are prepared to handle this type of hardship. When we encounter these types of circumstances, our initial reaction is to feel as if we have been ambushed by life.

Though all of us become temporarily overloaded at times by life's circumstances, most of us find a way to manage. It is when there is a convergence of life circumstances extended over time that we can begin a downward spiral of becoming emotionally disconnected.

This chronic state of being overwhelmed feels like we are dying emotionally inside. To die emotionally means that we experience the fears of failure, rejection, and abandonment at the same time and with the same intensity. We become emotionally overloaded to the point that we become like a walking, lifeless zombie.

When we are not dealing with our fears of failure, rejection, and abandonment, we automatically become emotionally handicapped. To become emotionally handicapped means that the degree and amount of unresolved pain in our lives significantly outweighs the pain we have resolved. Like a scuba diver with weights walking along the ocean floor who must release the weights in order to come to the surface, so we need to release the weights of failure, rejection, and abandonment. Otherwise, we will find our life source of oxygen running out, causing us to feel like we are dying emotionally. If this happens, we either withdraw or wait for others to take responsibility for our unwillingness to deal with our pain.

Over the years we have seen many life situations where the quality and intensity of verbal or physical abuse over an extended period of time caused a spouse, child, or single adult to feel like life had been drained from his or her soul. To be constantly told you are a failure, to have your thoughts rejected combined with consistent threats of abandonment creates an emotional overload. Individuals will respond by either becoming entrapped or by courageously escaping and finding healing for the pain.

Fear of Dying Physically

Anna lived a secure and simple life. Monday through Friday she drove to a local doctor's office where she worked as a bookkeeper. She spoke to few people and ate her lunches alone.

She became troubled when she overheard a coworker talking about a rare disease she heard about on television. The symptoms Anna had been experiencing lately seemed to be the same as the symptoms the coworker was talking about. Anna went to her doctor for a full examination, and much to her surprise the doctor found nothing. Anna's only consolation was that at least she didn't have that disease.

Yet for Anna, this began a period of searching for possible illnesses. When the local news did a special on the symptoms of a disease carried by mosquitoes, Anna felt she was a likely victim. When she saw a newspaper article on a woman dying from a rare blood disease, Anna researched the disease to learn all of the related symptoms. Each night she returned to her secluded apartment to scan the *Physicians Desk Reference* to find what diseases her bodily symptoms seemed to match.

She lived her days preoccupied with losing her good health. Her anxiety-driven tendencies to try to gather information and hound her doctors for information all centered around her dread that she was going to suffer the kind of death her mother—who died when Anna was in grade school—suffered. Her mother died from a rare form of cancer that doctors were able to diagnose only after an autopsy. Anna feared she had an unusual illness that would cause her to suffer the same fate as her mother.

The Ultimate Finality

Unlike the fear of dying emotionally, the fear of dying physically is an inevitable reality we must all face. We will die. Almost daily the newspapers, television, and movies depict people dying and being brutally murdered. But death's stark reality hits hardest when either a loved one or a friend dies or has a life-threatening illness. At these crossroads, we are forced to face our own vulnerability. "Human beings are naturally anxious because we are ultimately helpless and abandoned in a world where we are fated to die," explains Sam Keen. Anna's constant search to find a possible disease was a frantic way to deal with the reality of her own mortality.

Our lives consist of a multitude of beginnings and endings, ebbs and flows. We find that when one stage of life ends a new one begins, except in the case of dying. Death is ultimate finality and haunts us of our own finiteness.

It is what we cannot see with our human eyes that makes the terror of death so overwhelming. We become afraid of how long we will live, how we will die, and what will happen after we die. We try to alleviate this fear by fooling ourselves into thinking that if we take the right vitamins, eat the right foods, and live a balanced lifestyle we will be able to postpone the inevitable.

In his book *Denial of Death,* Ernest Becker proposed that since death is so overpowering, we create schemes to keep it out of our conscious thinking. We defend against this fear by participating in something of lasting worth.[8] If we begin a family, accumulate money, write a book, speak to millions, or make a scientific discovery, we believe we have taken care of our horror of dying. While any of these activities may help humanity for the greater good, they never take away our terror of being unable to control our own destinies.

Signs of the Fear of Death

For those of us who struggle with this fear of death—either emotional or physical death—several of the following signs may appear:

- Becoming preoccupied with our health and the possibility of illness.
- Becoming obsessed with the thought that a loved one might die.
- Never being at peace.
- Trying to live good lives to "please" God and thereby lengthen the days of our lives.
- Unwilling to take trips for fear of an accident.
- Becoming preoccupied with thoughts of heaven and hell.
- Being unable to celebrate the good things in our lives.
- Feeling often discouraged and at times despairing.
- Becoming emotionally numb.
- Remaining emotionally distant in relationships.

It takes strength to confront our fear of death. It is only when we truly look this fear in the face that we begin to start living. We cannot celebrate our life until we have come to peace with our death. In light of the inevitability of our own deaths, all the petty annoyances slip away. In that perspective we find ourselves living for the truly great things in life.

Author Iris Murdoch writes in her novel *The Nice and The Good* about a man who is in a critical life-threatening situation. He is trapped in a cave, waist-deep in water. Soon the water will rise above him. He thinks, "If I ever get out of here I will be no man's judge . . . not to judge, not to be superior, not to exercise power, not to seek, seek, seek. To love and to reconcile and to forgive, only this matters. All power is sin and all law is frailty. Love is the only justice. Forgiveness, reconciliation, not law."[9]

As we have examined the various types of fear, we can see that none of us is exempt from experiencing one or more of these fears: failure, rejection, abandonment, or death. Each day of our lives we may be confronted with any of these fears. The issue isn't how we will keep ourselves from feeling these emotions, but whether we will learn to manage our fears or let our fears manage us.

Steps in Overcoming Our Fears

Do the thing you fear to do and keep
on doing it . . . that is the quickest
and surest way ever yet discovered
to conquer fear.

❖

DALE CARNEGIE

Every job requires a set of skills to accomplish the task at hand. For instance, if the pipes under the kitchen sink begin to leak and you're not a plumber and can't afford one, you must buy a book on home plumbing to figure out how to fix it. Without the knowledge and skill, you won't know which end of the wrench to use or which size of piping to buy; that leak continues. The same is true in learning how to manage our fears. We need to be willing to roll up our sleeves and apply ourselves to the principles of learning how to resolve our fears.

In this chapter we will look at the key factors that have to be considered in order to master our fears: learning to become a risk-taker, developing supportive relationships, making a commitment to growth and change, and growing in faith by developing an eternal perspective.

Learn to Be a Risk-Taker

"To risk means you have to be willing to get out of the boat. We must be willing to leave our mundane existence. You cannot grow without risk and you cannot risk without sometimes failing," author and teacher John Ortberg states.

Consider something as simple and supposedly fun as telling a joke. There's risk involved. Jim told a joke and just as he reached the punch line he forgot the ending. Mortified, he wished he could somehow evaporate. He resolved in his mind that he will never take that risk again. A few minutes later, Annie told a joke and forgot the punch line also. She regained her composure and said, "There I go again. Another menopause moment."

This time, everyone laughs, tension is released, and the blunder is soon forgotten—especially by Annie, who tells another joke soon after and this time remembers the punch line.[1]

Jim and Annie's conclusions in the middle of an embarrassing situation were significant in their own growth. Jim saw the situation as so mortifying that he resolved to never tell a joke again, while Annie chose to lighten the tension, which freed her up to risk again.

Learning from Setbacks

Being willing to risk means digging down deep into our souls and saying, "No matter what, I am going to take a chance. I am going to just do it." Michael Jordan, considered by many the greatest basketball player ever to play the sport, once gave his "secret of success." In a commercial for a famous maker of athletic shoes, Michael said in a calm voice, "I've missed more than 9,000 shots in my career. I've lost more than 300 games. Twenty-six times I've been trusted to make the game winning shot—and missed. I've failed over and over and over again in my life. And that is why I succeed."[2]

We can feel the confidence in his voice. We definitely saw that confidence on the basketball court. When Michael felt afraid, rather than be immobilized by his fear, he pushed through it by trying again.

How do you handle your fears? Do you push through again and again, knowing that you can't "make every basket"? Do you know in your heart that you gave it your best shot? It's all about attitude and perspective—the attitude that "I can do anything I put my mind to." No, that doesn't mean we will have a perfect score or will not fail. It does mean we have a confidence that our honest attempts are in and of themselves a sign of success by the fact that we have actually tried.

Learning to Try Again

Jonas Salk made 200 attempts to discover the polio vaccine. When someone asked him how it felt to fail 200 times, his quick reply was, "I have never failed at anything in my life. I just figured out 200 ways how not to make the polio vaccine."

Winston Churchill was asked what most prepared him to lead Great Britain during World War II. He responded by saying, "It was the time I had to repeat a grade in elementary school." The reporter questioned him further. "You mean you flunked a grade?" Without skipping a beat he said, "I never failed a grade in my life. I was given a second chance to get it right."

We can see from their perspectives that these men didn't allow their fears to minimize their desire to succeed. It is how we react to the events in our lives that counts.

Failure can be our teacher—teaching us to grow in wisdom. Unless we try and risk failing, we will never learn those excellent ways of becoming the strong, honest, loving persons that God created us to be. "Your instincts tell you to escape or avoid," says Steven Philipson, clinical director of the Center for Cognitive-Behavioral Psychotherapy in New York City. "But what you really need to do is face down the fear. When you spend your life in a cautionary crouch, the greatest relief of all may come from simply standing up."[3]

For all of the research and writing on building one's self-esteem, it is interesting to note that the single most significant factor in building self-esteem is simply facing difficult situations head-on. When we avoid, refuse to take a chance, squirm away from coming up to the plate, we are basically saying to ourselves, *I don't have what it takes.* However, when we take a risk and try something we have never attempted before, we grow in our understanding of our abilities and ourselves. We learn more about our natural and self-imposed limitations. As we take risks, we realize how we might have perceived a situation inaccurately or had underestimated our own abilities. If we take a risk and fail, we can at least say that we found the nerve to try. It is at those times we find ourselves growing in courage because we can say, "I rose to the challenge."

Learning to Be Real

When we face our fears, we not only learn to risk, grow in wisdom, and build our self-esteem, but we also learn that we don't need to pretend to be someone we are not. We are free to admit that we are like everyone else in the human race. We don't have to play the role of an impostor. We then find the freedom to be who we are with all of our unique abilities. We learn what it means to be real.

In the classic children's book *The Velveteen Rabbit,* Margery Williams described what it means to become real through two children's toy characters.

"What is REAL?" asked the Rabbit one day, when they were lying side by side near the nursery fender, before Nana came to tidy the room. "Does it mean having things that buzz inside you and a stick-out handle?"

"Real isn't how you are made," said the Skin Horse. "It's a thing that happens to you. When a child loves you for a long, long time, not just to play with, but REALLY loves you, then you become REAL."

"Does it hurt?" asked the Rabbit.

"Sometimes," said the Skin Horse, for he was always truthful. "When you are Real you don't mind being hurt."

"Does it happen all at once, like being wound up," he asked, "or bit by bit?"

"It doesn't happen all at once," said the Skin Horse. "You become. It takes a long time. That's why it doesn't often happen to people who break easily, or have sharp edges, or who have to be carefully kept. Generally, by the time you are Real, most of your hair has been loved off, and your eyes drop out and you get loose in the joints and very shabby. But these things don't matter at all, because once you are Real you can't be ugly, except to people who don't understand."[4]

To risk is to be given the opportunity to be real. To be real is to ultimately live a life of freedom and to humbly accept all of who we are—the good, the bad, and the yet to become.

Develop Supportive Relationships

Someone to Cheer Us On

The second way to master our fears is by having supportive relationships. When we experience any one of the four major fears—failure, rejection, abandonment, or fear of dying—we need someone to say, "It's OK. You're going to make it." We need each other. Healthy relationships help soothe our sense of aloneness when we are facing down fear. When someone believes in us—in our abilities—and worth, it can give us the boost we need to overcome those things that scare us the most. We all need coaches who can help us see how we can succeed.

In our work with couples and individuals, we see real change and growth come more quickly when a loved one cheers them on. No matter what the fear is, when someone is standing beside us and communicating his or her faith in us, we are given the strength to stand.

This type of strength comes to a wife as her husband reaches for her hand and communicates a confidence that she can face the abuse of her childhood. It comes to a dad when he sees his family gathered in the living room telling him that they believe he can overcome his addiction. And it comes to a woman, embraced by her best friend, as she weeps over the death of her child. In these situations and others like them, we are given an extra measure of faith, hope, and love to continue.

Words That Affirm

Counselor and author H. Norman Wright has reported an interesting tradition carried out by the Babemba tribe in southern Africa, one that helps members deal with their fears of rejection.

> Each person in the tribe who acts irresponsibly or unjustly is taken alone to the center of the village. Everyone in the village stops work and gathers in a large circle around the accused. In turn, each person in the tribe—regardless of age— speaks to the individual, recounting aloud the good things he has done in his lifetime. All the positive incidents in the per-

son's life, plus his good attributes, strengths, and kindness, are recalled with accuracy and detail.

Not one word about his irresponsible or antisocial behavior is shared. The ceremony, which sometimes lasts several days, isn't complete until every positive expression has been given by those assembled. At the conclusion of the ceremony, the person is welcomed back into the tribe. Can you imagine the feelings this person experiences during the tribe's welcome? Can you imagine how you would feel if a group of people affirmed you in that way?[5]

This tribal community knows the power of affirmation. At times we can become so narrowly focused in our perception of who we are, that all we see are our shortcomings and disappointments. We need people to speak words of encouragement. We need love that brings life, truth, and beauty into our darkened hearts.

When our son and daughter were young, I (Ray) would say to them every day, "I love you just because of who you are. You are lovable and huggable." Often I'd ask them later in the day, "How come I love you so much?" Each would perk up and say, "You love me just for who I am, lovable and huggable."

One day when Krista was about eight years old, I asked her the question, and she answered: "Daddy, you love me just for who I am, lovable and huggable." Then she added: "I love Jesus, and you are my bud."

My heart immediately filled with tenderness. I hugged her and said, "Isn't it great that we can love each other?"

I learned something very important that day. When you pour love into a person's soul with words of affirmation that say you love her (or him), that person is able to take that energy of love and transform it into new and different expressions of love back to others. Words not only affirm; they literally transform us into loving people who can more powerfully connect with others.

Make a Commitment to Growth

The Challenge of Change

A very important dimension in dealing with one's fears is to commit to growth and change. As counselors, we have had clients come into our office who say they want to deal with their fears but don't want to make the hard choices and changes to grow. In reality, they just want to feel better. They are not interested in doing the hard work of growth. We have also seen clients who have encountered experiences that had the potential to be emotionally crippling and have resolved to face their pain and grow.

A commitment to growth and change means we are steadfast in putting our whole hearts and minds into learning the principles that will aid us in dealing with our fears. "Life is three quarters learning how to deal with fear and one quarter learning to love," states Nell Thomas. We need to become experts at understanding and overcoming the fears that can undo us.

Five Stages of Growth

Just as a toddler needs to go through the crawling stage before she can walk, we must go through certain stages in order to change. The growth process has five stages. Each stage builds on the other. We must proceed through each stage in order to see deep, lasting change in our lives.

The first stage is our being aware of feeling anxiety or fear. Many people know something is wrong, yet they may not be sure just what it is. For example, Jill may be aware that she is afraid only when she is with her boss, but she does not really know why. In this stage, one is only vaguely aware of what the problem is.

The second stage is finding insight as to what we are afraid of. We move into becoming objective observers of our own intentions and behaviors. The goal is to find reasons for our behavior and feelings. In this stage Jill may realize that when she is with her boss she's so afraid of his evaluation that she refuses to think, instead retreating inside herself.

Having insight and awareness alone will not alter lifelong patterns. In order to change, there must be a high level of commitment to choosing a new way of being. That's *the third stage: We resolve to turn our insights into action.* Of all the stages, this stage is the most significant. This stage involves deciding to take a risk and move in new directions. Jill, for instance, may decide that she is tired of always cowering around her boss and wants to do something about it. Many people become stuck in this stage because it involves breaking out of old ways of living—ways that though often unhealthy, still have some degree of familiarity and safety.

The fourth stage is exploring new ways of responding. We have fully realized how our past ways of managing a situation have brought little success, and we explore new behaviors. In addition, in this stage we explore new ways of reacting and thinking. Thus Jill decides that the next time she is alone with her boss she will remind herself of her own capabilities and successes. She also will try to see her boss in a different light, as a human being with gifts and foibles like her own.

The final stage is the change stage. Here we enjoy the rewards of the hard work of growth, and see success and change in ourselves and in our world.

Grow in Faith with an Eternal Perspective

Fear is like a debilitating disease that penetrates our minds until it destroys all productive thoughts and renders us incapable of clear thinking. If we want to have relationships marked by intimacy and vulnerability, we need to face down the nagging voices that say we will never be accepted for who we are. Fear not only destroys our relationships with others but profoundly affects our ability to see God more clearly and grow in our faith.

Like a mountain climber scaling a flat-surfaced rock at 5,000 feet, we are virtually incapable of being able to enjoy the beauty of God's creation when we are focused on fear. An eternal perspective gives us the foundation to look out beyond our present circumstances and see the blessings we have been given.

Faith Is . . .

Faith is believing in a Creator God who loves us and accepts us. Faith is believing in a God who ultimately desires us to grow in becoming all of who He created us to be. Faith is believing that God does work all things out for our good and His glory. Faith is believing that this world is only a faint glimpse of all that heaven will be.[6] Revelation 21:1–4 speaks to this notion, indicating that one day God will call us to Himself, and we will live with Him forever. "He will wipe every tear from their eyes. There will be no more death or mourning or crying or pain" (verse 4). Therefore, an eternal perspective flows out of these foundational beliefs and assists us in rising above our present fears.

An eternal perspective says, "I am not alone in this vast universe, even though I might feel lonely and alienated and hurt by others." To be lonely is very different from being alone together with God. When we choose to develop a personal relationship with our Creator God in Christ Jesus, we then have at our disposal all the resources of heaven to encourage us during our times of trouble.

Over the years, we have said to our clients and friends that it has not been our psychology that has gotten us through our most difficult moments; it has been our faith in God. Jesus Christ said, "Come to me, all you who are weary and burdened, and I will give you rest. Take my yoke upon you and learn from me, for I am gentle and humble in heart, and you will find rest for your souls" (Matthew 11:28–29). We found great comfort in knowing that during times of great pain Jesus was right there with us desiring to carry our burdens.

Not only that, during our eleven "wilderness years," we knew we could trust that no matter what fear would threaten us, God's love for us was more powerful. The apostle Paul put it this way: "For I am convinced that neither death nor life, neither angels nor demons, neither the present nor the future, nor any powers, neither height nor depth, nor anything else in all creation, will be able to separate us from the love of God that is in Christ Jesus our Lord" (Romans 8:38–39).

Faith Chases Worry and Gives Rest

Faith teaches us to yield, release, and trust. Faith also tells us that all the worrying in the world will not add a single second to our lives. Jesus spoke to this when He said,

"Therefore I tell you, do not worry about your life, what you will eat or drink; or about your body, what you will wear. Is not life more important than food, and the body more important than clothes? Look at the birds of the air; they do not sow or reap or store away in barns, and yet your heavenly Father feeds them. Are you not much more valuable than they? Who of you by worrying can add a single hour to his life? Therefore do not worry about tomorrow, for tomorrow will worry about itself. Each day has enough trouble of its own." (Matthew 6:25–26, 34)

When we choose to rest in God's love, fear is not able to take residence in our soul. When we manage our fears of failure, rejection, abandonment, and death by increasing our faith, we open the floodgates of God's love. We find we can rest in the fact that God can be trusted to take care of all that concerns us. This is the antidote to the fear. Indeed, as the Scripture says, "Perfect love drives out fear" (1 John 4:18).

An eternal perspective helps us override our present fears to reach out to those around us. We find that our emotional energy is no longer sapped by anxiety. Our faith in God then not only strengthens us but becomes a catalyst to help those who are in need.

Our hope flows out of a belief that we can trust God's love, protection, and guidance in our lives. When we embrace this, we are liberated to live as messengers of God's love and goodwill to His children. To be filled with faith in God, have the hope of an eternal perspective, and be filled with His love to share freely with others can then defeat our fears of failure, rejection, abandonment, and death.

Through the Valley of the Kwai is a book written by Ernest Gordon of life in a World War II Japanese prison camp. Gordon wrote about a man named Angus McGillivray.

Angus was a strong, brawny Scottish prisoner in the prisoner of war camp. The camp had deteriorated into a demoralizing place. Men lived by the rule of the jungle—survival of the fittest. Acts of meanness and suspicion were the order of the day. Men were stealing from and cheating each other. They would have their personal belongings stolen right from under their heads as they were sleeping. The war camp had become a jungle of unleashed human depravity.

It was custom for the Scottish soldiers to have a "mucker," a friend with whom he shared or "mucked in" everything he had. It was becoming evident to everyone that Angus's mucker was slowly dying. Everyone had given up on him—except for Angus. At one point someone stole his mucker's blanket, so

Angus gave him his own. At mealtimes Angus would get rations and take them to his mucker, stand over him, and force him to eat. Going hungry was difficult for Angus because he was a man with such a big frame. Angus did everything in his power to see that his buddy survived. In time Angus's mucker got better.

Then one day, Angus collapsed, slumped over, and died. When the doctors examined him, they discovered he had died of starvation complicated by exhaustion. Angus had been giving of his own food, shelter, and energy to his beloved mucker. He had given everything for him—to the point of his very own life.

As word spread of what Angus McGillivray had done, the atmosphere of the camp began to change. His sacrificial actions had given the men an inspiration of how they were to live. Men began to focus not only on helping each other but sacrificing for each other as well. They shared their talents with each other. A cobbler and an engineer together created an artificial leg for amputees. One prisoner was a violinmaker, another an orchestra leader. Within time the camp had an orchestra full of homemade instruments. The men started gatherings where they could teach each other history, philosophy, and mathematics. A library was formed where they would make known to each other the books they had and arranged by word of mouth to pass them to others. A church was formed, named the "Church Without Walls," that was so powerful, so compelling, that a spirit of worship pervaded the camp. The prisoner of war camp that once was a place of dehumanizing depravity became a place that was transformed into a sanctuary of love—all because one man named Angus gave all he had for love.[7]

"Greater love has no one than this, that he lay down his life for his friends," Jesus said (John 15:13). What would compel Angus to give his life away for the sake of his friend? We believe Angus had a taste of eternity that blew apart all of his earthly fears of his own survival—and Angus left a taste of heaven to each of his fellow prisoners in the camp.

Fear and Control

It seems easier to be God than to
love God, easier to control people
than love people.

·:·

HENRI NOUWEN

What happens when fear gets the best of us and we cannot defeat it? What happens when we find ourselves
feeling overcome with constant worry? We try to control everything around us to minimize our anxiety.

Have you ever said one of these statements: "I feel like my
world is spinning out of control"; "You need to quit controlling me and let me decide how I will use my time"; or "Wow,
I have finally regained control of my life"?

Control is a word that evokes strong emotions when we hear
it. When we think of control, it stirs up feelings of power and
vulnerability, autonomy and conformity, gaining and losing.

The American Heritage Dictionary defines *control* as, "To exercise
authoritative or dominating influence over; to hold in restraint;
to regulate, to influence, to master, to restrain."

Our focus in this book has been on being able to move from fear to love. Fear that's not properly managed often leads to controlling behaviors and attitudes. Yet those who respond this way find themselves unable to love others well.

We move into the coping mechanism of control when we falsely believe that if we just manage our circumstances correctly we will not have any reason to feel afraid. Consequently, the woman who is afraid of her house being burglarized tries to control her fear by hiring a premier security company to watch her house twenty-four hours a day. The man who is afraid of not having enough money controls every penny his wife spends.

We will examine the positive as well as the detrimental aspects of control in our lives.

The Positive Aspects of Control

We all want to be in charge and know that by the choices we make we can reach our goals and positively affect the world around us. The mother exerts control when she grabs her young son from being hit by a car as he rushes into the street after his ball. The overweight woman who refuses to eat sugar and high-fat foods feels good about regaining control over her eating habits.

Increased Security

In a 1991 study, researcher David Katerndahl found that people struggling with panic attacks improved when they felt an increasing sense of control over their lives versus being subject to the control of events around them.[1]

With the life-threatening nature of cancer, it's not surprising that patients with breast cancer can feel helpless and without control. This loss of control is related to anxiety, depression, and poor prognosis among cancer patients. Similarly, studies have shown that individuals diagnosed with breast cancer who felt a sense of control over the treatment and the outcome of the disease were able to maintain a sense of well-being.[2]

In his book *The Pursuit of Happiness,* David Myers concluded that people who feel, for the most part, in control of their lives are happy and experience a sense of well-being.[3]

We need a sense of healthy control. Fear has its place to alert us to possible danger. Control has its place to help us feel a sense of security in our lives. When we exert control, we feel in charge of our environment and ourselves. Research has indicated the more self-mastery or control of our impulses we feel, the greater our self-esteem and the better able we are to face life's difficulties.

The Marshmallow Test

Years ago, researchers did a long-term study on personal self-control. Several four-year-olds were each given a marshmallow. In "the marshmallow test," the tester proposed the following: "You can eat the marshmallow immediately. Or, if you wait until I return, you will be permitted to eat two." Then the tester left the room.

Some four-year-olds grabbed the marshmallow within seconds of the tester leaving. Others rose to the challenge and waited fifteen to twenty minutes until the tester returned, receiving their well-earned reward. When these children were evaluated in adolescence, researchers found that the children who received the two marshmallows were "more socially confident, more personally effective, and better able to cope with the frustrations of life." Those who grabbed for the marshmallows tended as teenagers to "[shy] away from social contacts; to be stubborn and indecisive, to be easily upset by frustrations; to think of themselves as 'bad' or unworthy."[4]

In short, no matter who we are and what we are dealing with, having a sense of control reduces our stress, gives us a greater personal satisfaction, and improves our overall quality of life.

The Negative Aspects of Control

When does control become a problem? It becomes a problem when we have gone overboard in compensating against the things we fear rather than dealing with our fears head-on. In his book *The Control Freak,* Les Parrot addresses this notion. "Most people would agree that a sense of control is necessary for good emotional and physical health. But when people use control to dominate everything around them—other people, their environment, all situations, and circumstances—then they have crossed the boundary into overcontrol. The key is being smart enough to know when to use your control and when not to."[5]

Control becomes a problem when we are unable to adjust to our surroundings. When we feel we must always be in charge of events, others, and ourselves to take care of our fears, we have moved from healthy control to "controlling" behavior. This is when we believe that to survive in this world we must control everything around us. We mistakenly think that if we don't take charge, everything around us will fall apart.

Choosing to be controlling is like becoming a prisoner in our own soul. We become locked up emotionally and quite literally create a dividing wall between ourselves and others. Because we feel we must be in charge of everything, we are not open to the feedback and ideas of others (or perhaps only if they agree with us). Yet at the same time we are hypersensitive to their perceptions, which only intensifies our feelings of anxiety and the need to control. We may isolate ourselves from others, thinking that lesser contact will minimize our own personal stress. We can then become trapped in our own thought patterns, which inevitably leads us to dead-end conclusions.

When we are controlling, we feel a combination of anxiety and depression, causing us to feel trapped in our negative feelings. Physically, we can run ourselves into the ground because of the emotional energy spent on managing our anxiety. Typically we feel worn down; in response, we may sleep a lot, eat a lot, or become hypervigilant in the discipline of our bodies and our behavior.

The devastating effects of controlling behavior is seen in the life of Norman Garey, a powerful Hollywood lawyer described by author Elizabeth Brenner.

Los Angeles magazine featured an article about Norman Garey, one of the most powerful lawyers in Hollywood. His clients included Marlon Brando, Tony Curtis, and Gene Hackman; he was admired by friends and clients alike for his cool and his self control. A friend said, "He liked having an effect on people, being in control." . . . Garey was so well controlled, in fact, only his family knew about his struggle with depression and his growing dependence on psychiatric medication. Struggling with the relentless stress of life in the Hollywood fast lane, Garey found it more and more difficult to keep himself in control—yet he could not allow himself to lose it. Finally, he was caught in a deadlocked negotiation—his opponent refused to budge on several major points, and Garey faced the possibility of losing a lot of status and a lot of money. Depressed, desperate, but still "in control," he shot himself in the head with a .38-caliber Smith and Wesson revolver. After his death a friend said, "Norman Garey was not walking around like a crazy man. He didn't exhibit signs of depression. He was always the model of organization, awareness, and control."[6]

How We Control; Why We Control

Doing It My Way

If there were a theme song for controlling people, it would be "My Way" by Frank Sinatra. Everywhere we turn, we can see people seizing the opportunities to control others. A mother controls her son by telling him where to walk when he attempts to cross the street. A wife wants more affection from her husband, so she controls him by withholding sex. A husband controls his wife's choices and behavior by allowing her a small amount of money each week for groceries and shopping. An adolescent holds the family hostage with her negative attitudes toward everything and everybody.

We become most afraid of the things we cannot control. For instance, Susie eats well, gets plenty of rest, and takes her vitamins so she won't have to worry about her health. But when Laura, who sits at the next desk, comes to work coughing and hacking with a nasty case of the flu, Susie begins to panic, because she knows there is little she can do to avoid the possibility of getting sick.

Using Control as a Counterbalance

There is a law in physics that any force will have an equal and opposite reaction. For example, observe a large crane lifting materials to the upper floors of a newly constructed building, and you will notice the crane is designed to counterbalance the weight it is lifting by having large weights placed at the opposite end of the crane. This law also applies to the dynamics of fear and control: The force and weight of our fears can cause us to counterbalance with control. When we become afraid, like the lifting of materials, we automatically and intuitively respond by controlling our environment.

The more intense the stress and the stronger the pressures, the more fearful we become. The more afraid we become, the more we counterbalance ourselves by becoming more controlling. That is why it is so important for each of us to take good care of ourselves emotionally by working hard to resolve our fears. If we don't, we will inevitably counterbalance our fear by becoming more controlling.

This seeking of control makes sense; we have seen too many experiences where someone was vulnerable and something painful occurred. A woman who sees a horrific shooting in a restaurant determines that she will always carry a handgun in her purse so that she can protect herself if she is ever in that situation again. An adult once teased in fourth grade for being stupid drives himself to eventually get his doctorate so that he will always be seen as smart.

A friend who is an avid golfer informs us that the principles of golf are all about control. If the golfer overcontrols his swing, his contact with the ball will result in a hook, slice, or just topping the ball. He says the major goal of every golfer is to establish a consistent swing that will guarantee a fairway shot.

A good golf pro can detect how a golfer's stance and swing will cause him/her to overcontrol. Just as there are golfing styles, so it is with those who are controlling. As in the game of golf, so it is in the game of life. We need to understand the ways we try to control. There are four controlling types of people: They are the power controllers, pride controllers, passive controllers, and protective controllers. Each displays a distinctive style while trying to control his or her environment. Let's look at each.

Four Styles of Controlling People

Traits of Power Controllers

It is easy to spot power controllers. They're the people who maneuver their way into positions of dominance to manipulate and control others. They feed on the adrenaline rush that comes with influential positions. An executive at a large company described his boss and CEO by stating, "The difference between God and Harold is that God does not believe He is Harold." Their primary motivation in life is to quench their fears, whether of failure, rejection, abandonment, or death. Power controllers deal with their fears by moving into positions of dominance over others.

Power controllers tend to be goal-oriented and bottom-line driven. They are not team players and would rather be the leaders of others. At times they appear aloof and cold. Typically, they see the people around them as pieces in a chess game to be strategically moved and manipulated rather than valued and respected.

Power controllers are relentless and ruthless in their pursuit of victory. Games are not games but tests of their ability to conquer and win. Their need to triumph over others is driven by their need to maintain their magical feelings of invincibility.

Parents as Power Controllers

When a father or mother uses the power controller tactics in a family, the results can be devastating.

Martin described dinnertime with his family as something out of the movie *The Godfather*. He recalled how the family would sit down at the table and not speak a word until his father would open the conversation. His father would choose a topic for discussion, like politics, and would only recognize those who would agree with his view. His father would censure family members who dared to disagree with him by stony silence and a cold stare. Martin's father would manipulate the family both verbally and nonverbally.

As a controller, his dad used nonverbal power messages as simple as a lack of eye contact to a cold, glaring intense look.

His power approach has affected Martin's relationships as an adult. "I guess I learned to anticipate seeing relationships based on competition," Martin explains. "Now I can't seem to trust anybody—even my own kids. Even today I find myself acting like my own dad; I find myself being critical and judgmental to my own family."

The power of those fears in Martin's life has resulted in broken relationships with his own adult children. People like Martin learn to compensate for their fears and inadequacies by using power as a tool to control others. In the end, Martin's fear cost him love.

Power Controllers and Influence

For power controllers, knowledge becomes a tool to be used to gain influence over others. They work hard getting into the right graduate schools in order that their training will afford them that prestigious position with the right firm, medical practice, or tenured faculty position. They realize that the right academic degree combined with the best job afford them both influence and wealth. They work hard to become the leaders of their selected fields and to collect the materialistic badges of honor, profiled in the cars they drive, houses they buy, country clubs they join, and organizations they strive to lead.

Eli Black, former chief executive officer of The United Fruit Company, who tragically ended his life by suicide, was a good example of a power controller. Tom McCann, vice president of public relations at United Fruit Company at the time Black was CEO, wrote about Black in the book *An American Company.* McCann explained that when Black initially came to the United Fruit Company, Black's primary concern was to establish himself as a person of incredible charisma and power. McCann specifically recalls his first face-to-face introduction to Black at a meeting that he and two other vice presidents had with Black at a Boston restaurant.

As we sat down at the table, Black smiled and asked if we were hungry. I had come into the office early that morning and had missed breakfast, so I smiled back and told him that I was starving. A moment later a busboy arrived with a plate of cheese and crackers. Before the plate touched the table, Black reached over and took it from the busboy's hand. At first I was certain he was going to pass it around the table, but instead he placed it right in the center of his own place setting, then clasped his hands in front of it. "Now," he said, still unsmiling, "what's on the agenda?"

For the next several minutes, Johnson and Lauer [the two other vice presidents] talked with Black about the building in San Jose [Costa Rica]. . . . I added a comment here and there, keeping my eye on the cheese and crackers. The only way I could get one, other than by asking for it, would be to reach across Black's arm; and Black was making it very clear by the way he positioned himself directly over my quarry that to violate his territory in that matter would be a serious breach of etiquette. I sat back for a few minutes longer, weighing the demands of my neglected stomach against the possible consequences to my career. Finally, when Black still showed no signs of action, I found a brief pause in the discussion and I said, "How about some cheese and crackers, Eli?"

Black was looking at Lauer, and when I asked the question he never even glanced in my direction. It crossed my mind that the request had not registered, so I decided to rephrase it and I tried again.[7]

He continued the conversation about Costa Rica, and McCann tried, with some success, to ignore his stomach and enter the conversation. Black, in turn, talked to the other VPs. Then, while asking Lauer some more questions, Black gathered soft cheese onto his knife, picked up a round cracker from the plate, and, as McCann described it,

> poised the cracker on his fingertips as he carefully stroked a rounded, tantalizing mound of cheese spread over its face.
>
> The cracker remained balanced on the fingertips of Black's left hand for at least the next five minutes. He asked Lauer questions about the height of the building from the street and its height above sea level. He asked about the color and materials of the facade, about the use of each floor, about the size of the lobby . . . My eyes never left the cracker. . . .
>
> I leaned back again, this time accepting my defeat.[8]

Only then, when McCann had ended his protests, did Black reach across the table and place the cracker on McCann's butter plate. The rest of the food the CEO kept "within his embrace, for him alone to dispense or to keep."

This story is a compelling illustration depicting what happens when a person chooses to use his power to dominate others. On one level Black's actions seem trivial. On another level Black clearly demonstrated to McCann and the other men at the table that he was obviously in charge and not to be contended with. Because of Black's self-assured, calculated demeanor, it is difficult to see how he was being motivated by fear. Yet behind this bravado was a man terrified of being seen as an impotent and uninspiring leader.

Surprisingly, power controllers are generally unaware of the fear that motivates their actions. They may describe their behavior as "strategic . . . knowing how to play the game," or simply "being in charge." Yet, underneath these self-descriptions is a disturbing fear of vulnerability and of their inadequacies being discovered. Power controllers become experts at minimizing their chances of getting sideswiped from others or events by jockeying for positions of dominance and supremacy.

What feelings do power controllers stir up in people around them? Intimidation, anger, insecurity. When we are in the presence of a power controller, we feel a combination of anger and insecurity. On one hand, we don't like being dominated. Yet, on the other hand, we feel uncertain in ourselves and how to deal with their power.

Traits of Pride Controllers

We can all remember seeing a two-year-old telling the parent, "It's mine; I want that. . . . Johnny has my toy." Being selfish and self-centered as a child is a stage we all go through and, for most of us, grow out of. A pride controller, simply stated, is a two-year-old in an adult body.

All personality types are a blend of each other. A power controller may have some of the pride controller traits. The power controller deals with fear by dominating while the pride controller deals with fear by needing to be glorified. The pride controller deals with fear by making sure that others admire him at the expense of his ability to be sensitive to others.

From a clinical perspective, we call these behaviors and attitudes *narcissistic*. The word *narcissism* comes from the Greek myth of Narcissus. The young man became so enamored with his reflection in a pool of water that he fell into the pond and drowned. Narcissism, then, refers to a vain preoccupation with oneself.

The pride controller tends to be self-absorbed and exhibits little ability to truly empathize with others. This type of controller moves in his or her world feeling entitled to special favors and privileges just because of who he is. This controller has an insatiable need to be affirmed and admired.

Michael MacCoby wrote about pride-controller behavior in a recent article in the *Harvard Business Review.* He noted the following behaviors of the pride controllers:

1. They are emotionally isolated individuals and are highly distrustful.
2. They fly into a rage at perceived threats.
3. They are extraordinarily sensitive to criticism as a whole and will not want to listen when feeling attacked.
4. They listen only for the kind of information they seek and don't learn easily from others.
5. They don't like to teach but prefer indoctrination and making speeches.
6. Paradoxically, even though they have extreme difficulty being empathetic, they personally crave empathy from others.[9]

Pride controllers know whom they can manipulate, and they use them for their own gain. Relationships are seen as something that is strictly for their needs and not for the benefit of others. In fact, pride controllers feel others are fortunate to be in relationship with them. Pride controllers are skilled at maintaining a relationship with some people while keeping others at arm's length.

We can identify the pride controllers by the people who seem "perfect" in everything they do. They are the people who seem to have no visible weaknesses or problems and in fact are many times quite gifted. Yet, pride controllers have no real sense of themselves and are consequently nothing but image.

Pride Controllers and Perceptions

Pride controllers want to make sure that people around them perceive them as superior and unique, possessing gifts and abilities that few others have. They move through their world with a sense of entitlement because they view themselves as special. Because they see themselves as special, they believe they are entitled to the best seats at the baseball game and preferential treatment at their favorite restaurant.

Pride controllers are always scanning their world to see how they are perceived and how those they associate with are perceived. They make sure their loved ones dress well, present well, and are at the top of the crowd competitively. For instance, a pride controller is not satisfied with her daughter making the traveling soccer team; she needs to be the star player of the team.

Like power controllers, pride controllers make sure they have achieved appropriate status, shown in designer clothes, well-appointed cars, and well-decorated homes. They are hypervigilant in their striving to be perfect in whatever they undertake. All of the behaviors and attitudes of the pride controller are clear indications of how they have counterbalanced their fear of insecurity and vulnerability.

Pride Controllers and the Marriage Relationship

The pride controller's behavior can have a devastating effect on his/her marriage. The self-centered and selfish attitudes and behaviors can cause this controller's spouse to feel like he or she is single but married. The pride controller's personality can create an atmosphere of isolation and alienation from those he or she loves; this controller can drive people away by his demands. The pride controller can wear people out, especially a spouse.

The brilliant artist Pablo Picasso fit this type of profile in his relationships. His mother cautioned his first wife, "I don't believe any woman could be happy with my son. He's available for himself but for no one else." Picasso was quoted as saying that there were only two types of women, "goddess and doormat," and eventually each of his wives and lovers would go from the first type to the second.

"When I die," Picasso declared, "it will be a shipwreck, and as when a huge ship sinks, many people all around will be sucked down with it." He was right: Upon his death both his second wife and an early mistress committed suicide, and his first wife and another mistress had psychiatric breakdowns. Typical of pride controllers, Picasso never realized the primitive, self-centered love for which he was longing. "I guess I'll die without ever being loved," he sadly conceded.[10]

Over the years we have worked with marriages where either one or both spouses exhibited strong pride-controlling attitudes. Again, such control traces back to one's efforts to deal with his or her fears.

People who are around the pride controller, including the spouse, have a number of reactions. They may feel inferior and then want to please the person to gain acceptance and approval. They can also feel a need to compete for the pride controller's affection. Over time people will feel manipulated and used and not valued as individuals in their own right. Their own fear of rejection may keep them with the pride controller, never realizing that fear is what motivates the pride controller also. They will either become stuck in a codependent posture or get tired of the constant emotional demands and leave the relationship.

Traits of Passive Controllers

How can someone be a passive controller? It appears to be an oxymoron. How can someone run away and be in control at the same time? We all know people who because of their anxieties and fears have put off completing reports on time, or instead of confronting a situation let the dynamics play out without any intervention on their part. Their passive nature makes them respond to their world with a stealthlike nature.

Yet they are in control—by being passive they have chosen what they believe is the most effective response. Passive controllers are present but unwilling to engage because they are scared of rejection and abandonment. We remember someone once saying, "I have two sets of people I relate to, my family and everyone else." He was clearly saying he keeps his distance from others so that he does not have to risk being hurt. He would not control his family through passivity (he did not fear them), but he would control others (he did fear them). The pain deflective shield that passive controllers raise is designed to protect them at all costs even if it means losing their friends, coworkers, or even family in the process. Their need for safety and security is paramount in their eyes.

Passive controllers are the least likely to be spotted—at least initially. These are the people who *appear* on the outside as the most easygoing individuals around. But on the inside they are so highly sensitive that it is as if they are equipped with highly tuned emotional radar that picks up on anything that may cause pain. They constantly scan their environment for potential hazards and harm.

Tactics of Passive Controllers

So how does a passive controller control? Simply as the name implies . . . by dodging anxiety-producing situations and letting others take responsibility. Passive controllers deal with their fears like ostriches do when sensing danger; they stick their heads in the sand and hope the danger will go away.

"I have finally figured out how to get along with my boss," Denise said, and she began to explain her boss's typical passive controller behavior. "Let's see. Where do I begin? I don't ask him about things he isn't well versed in or talk to him about situations that may involve conflict. I don't ask him when my next review is or whether I will get a pay increase or a task that I need direction in. If I attempt to talk about any of those topics, I can be guaranteed that he will avoid seeing me, not answer my voice mail, or return my E-mail. He never takes the initiative; I always have to."

As we can see with Denise's boss, a passive controller forces others to compensate for his or her anxieties.

Passive controllers become experts at steering clear of intimacy in relationships. They are courteous and respectful of others but are extremely guarded about getting close.

Passive controllers typically generate three responses in others. First, people around passive controllers question their own needs and worth. Because passive controllers do not want to discuss difficult situations and feelings, they leave people doubting if their requests were unreasonable or they are unimportant. Second, people around passive controllers often become angry at having to assume unwanted responsibility from the passive controllers's adept skills of avoiding difficult situations. Third, people dealing with passive controllers feel confused by the mixed messages being sent. On one hand, the controllers want to be in relationship with others and need people in their lives.

On the other hand, they want the relationship as long as they can guarantee acceptance and safety, a desire fueled by their constant fear. Consequently, those around passive controllers are unsure as to what kind of relationship the controller really wants.

Traits of Protective Controllers

Emily has reached the end of her rope. "Sometimes I feel like shaking my mom and shouting, 'Stop treating me like a child! Just let me grow up!'" Emily's mother is a classic worrier. "Even though I am living on my own, she will call me every morning to see that I have gotten up in time for work. In the evenings she will call and we go through Twenty Questions." Emily continues, "When I said something to her about wanting to be on my own, she says I am ungrateful for all she does for me."

Emily's mother is a protective controller. These controllers hover over their loved ones usually as a way of showing love and care. Yet the recipients of their concern experience them as being manipulative and dominating. It appears they are more interested in getting others to do what they want so they can feel better rather than actually helping others' lives to function better.

Protective controllers are motivated by their fear that their world could come apart. They believe they will not be able to survive if their loved ones are hurt. They have good intentions when they are controlling the people around them but are driven by their own fear and pain. The protective controllers work so hard at taking care of others because they are constantly fighting against their fears of failure, rejection, and abandonment. The intensity of these fears is in direct proportion to the amount of pain they have experienced in their lives.

Their childhood years have influenced profoundly how they view themselves and those they love. The core of their pain comes from experiences with mothers, fathers, siblings, and/or significant others, who, on various levels, hurt them deeply. This left them feeling poorly about themselves. It also left them with a decision to try to control their relationships so they can ensure they will not be hurt again. The net effect for these individuals is they developed a high need for feeling safe in relationships.

None of us wants to live under conditions of any kind that are harmful to others or ourselves. When we control, we behave in ways that ensure for us the highest amount of safety possible. Protective controllers mistakenly believe that if they handle everything in their life and the lives of others, they can ensure safety. This type of controller believes that people around him will not be able to function well unless he takes charge of their lives. The protective controller fears that the people he cares about will experience pain if he (or she) doesn't protect them.

Protective Controllers and Emotional Equilibrium

Protective controllers strive to maintain their emotional equilibrium. Their emotional equilibrium is thrown off when they think everything is going well, and all of a sudden, like a lightning bolt out of the sky, they experience unexpected pain. They diligently fight against hearing from others that they have failed or they are not appreciated for their acts of care. Like falling down the stairs, any of these experiences will throw protective controllers into a reactive state of wanting to fix the situation.

They need to keep all negative feelings to a minimum, desiring only to experience love and acceptance from others. The intensity of those needs is based in not having received the unconditional love they needed when they were younger. As adults they want their world to give them what they lacked when they were children.

145

Because of this unresolved pain, protective controllers tend to become very sensitive to revealing when they feel they have failed, fearing they could become abandoned altogether. What may appear to be originating in a need to dominate is really covering a desperate fear of vulnerability. The focal point of their control is their need to take care of their fears. Their underlying motivation is, *If I control others, then I won't be hurt and I can get what I need.*

That was Robert. He decided the type of clothes his wife would wear, the weekly menu, how the house would be decorated and with whom they would spend their social time.

When Dorothy joked about his making her into the woman he has always wanted, he chuckled and confessed that he is a control freak. When challenged as to why he is that way, he explained, "I grew up learning that you could only trust yourself. I have had enough pain in my life for two lifetimes! If I am in charge of everything, including those closest to me, I can be confident that my life will go well."

For Robert, the more he tried to control the people around him (particularly his wife)—their feelings and the events of their lives—the further out of reach they became.

Causes of Controlling Behavior

We can see from the various controlling styles how counterproductive controlling behavior can be. When we struggle with controlling behavior, there's stress for us and those we seek to control. To grow beyond these destructive patterns is to see that truly, no matter how much we might feel in charge of events and people around us, we are not ultimately in control.

Controlling behavior can appear due to any of the following three reasons:

1. We are afraid of failure, rejection, abandonment, or death.

2. We have a need or combination of needs that are not being met (that is, not being listened to or not being respected).

3. We have a set of desires that have been unfulfilled. The difference between a need and a desire is that our desires are an expression of how our needs will be met. For example, we all have a need to be loved. Some people desire that need to be shown through acts of kindness while others desire to hear words of affirmation.

Finding Freedom from Controlling Behavior

Generally, a key indicator that we are moving into controlling behavior or attitudes is when we find ourselves becoming irritated or angry. The challenge for all of us is to develop the skills to identify and express what our specific fears are before they get converted to anger. We also need to learn how to express our needs in such a way so our request is seen as an invitation to those we love—and not a demand. Lastly, we need to specifically tell others our desires as to how we would like our needs to be met.

Here are questions you might want to ask yourself if you have either identified that you are controlling or if someone has hinted, or told you clearly, that you are controlling.

- What do you perceive might happen if you are not in control of the situation or person?
- Reflect on what you are primarily afraid will happen. Are you afraid of rejection? Failure? Being abandoned?

Once you answer those questions, take the following steps to move away from controlling behavior:

1. Be aware of how you might wrongly feel responsible for others' behavior and emotional lives.

2. Identify what you can realistically control (i.e., your schedule, your eating habits, yourself).

3. Become more internally directed. Rather than focusing on your environment, focus on what you can change within yourself to find more peace.

4. Invite others to help you in your process of change. Ask someone you trust to help you identify when you are falling back into old patterns of control.

5. Invite honest feedback from others.

6. Walk in humility. Refuse to act in ways that position you in charge. Refuse to enter into power plays.

7. Realize that the patterns you established will take time to change.

8. Resolve not to be controlling about being controlling.

Releasing Control

We once heard an old Japanese fable that reminded us of our need to release our desires to control. A little boy found a tiny sparrow with a broken wing in the forest outside his home. The little boy took the bird inside and gently and lovingly nursed it back to health. He became so fond of the little bird; it became like a special friend.

Within time the little bird's wing healed. It would flap its wings wildly and throw itself against the bars of its cage. The boy's father saw this and said to him, "Son, it is time to let her go. She was made for the wild."

They carried the cage outside, and the boy gently lifted the bird from the cage. The tiny bird immediately sensed her freedom and began flapping its wings. The boy closed his hand, fearing that he would lose the tiny bird forever. The father turned to his son.

"My son," he said softly, "you must open your hand. I know you love her, but if you hold her tightly like this you may break her fragile wings."

"But if I open my hand she will fly away!" cried the boy.

"Perhaps," replied the father. "If you let her go she may return. But if you hold her tightly as you are you will surely lose her and harm her. The only way you can ever hold something wild and free is with an open hand."

This little boy painfully learned that to let go of control is to not only let go of our fears but also to make a choice to love. Whatever the type of control we or those we love may be dealing with, it takes great courage to let go of the need to control. It is only then we find we are beginning to learn how to love.

When Anger Supercharges Our Fears

We have met the enemy and he is us.

·:·

POGO (COMIC STRIP CHARACTER)

One Christmas we took some friends, who had never visited a city as large as Chicago, to Michigan Avenue to see the decorations. Known in the city as "The Magnificent Mile," Michigan Avenue was clogged with traffic, as might be expected. We were driving along when traffic suddenly stopped, leaving about one-third of our car blocking a driver who wanted to turn out onto the road. We moved up as far as we could without hitting the car in front of us.

Suddenly, without warning, the driver we were blocking went into a rage. When we finally were able to move up, he jumped out of his car, began screaming at us, and started viciously beating on our hood! Our friends' eyes became as large as saucers as they watched this man go through his tirade. It was difficult to convince them that this was not an everyday experience in Chicago! Somehow, our blocking this man's car in traffic became a trigger for him to let loose all of the built-up stress and anxiety in his life.

Though his reaction was extreme, most of us have had the experience of being cut off suddenly by another driver and feeling anger build up from within. Some of us use foul words, while others speak in a form of sign language featuring wild, unfriendly gestures. Once the danger has past, we immediately catch our breath and say, "I could have been killed if I hadn't swerved out of the way." When we realize this, our hearts race as we experience panic realizing what could have happened.

C. Leslie Charles, author of *Why Is Everyone So Cranky?* wrote, "We are overwhelmed, overworked, overscheduled and overspent. . . . Despite [having] families, good jobs, health, and numerous possessions, [we] feel isolated, alienated and ignored. Some have been chronically angry for so long they don't know how to let go of it, and they're afraid of what might happen if they do."[1] Anger has become a daily habit for most people. Fighting for our rights has become a priority over common courtesy.

From stressed-out students to overburdened postal workers, we are a society at the breaking point. With the onset of faxes, E-mail, beepers, and cell phones, there is little place to find relief. As one man stated, "All I want for Christmas is a phone-less cord."

"So-called road rage is a kind of culture tantrum," wrote Leon James, coauthor of *Road Rage and Aggressive Driving: Steering Clear of Highway Warfare*. He noted that "the way we express our anger . . . is culturally condoned or sanctioned."[2]

Fox-TV's *The Simpsons*, the pop satirical cartoon on our culture, aired an episode in which Marge, the matriarch of the ultimate dysfunctional family, found herself a perpetrator of road rage. She was driving in the family's new sport utility vehicle and became stuck behind a funeral procession. She veered out from behind the procession yelling, "Get that corpse off the road! The streets are for the living!" She was then pulled over, ticketed, and sent to traffic school. In the next scene, Marge is calmly listening to the course instructor, Sergeant Crew, telling the students, "So when you go out for a drive, remember to leave your murderous anger where it belongs—at home."

Anger: Rooted in Fear

Anger is an emotion that we experience on a variety of levels—from irritation to violent rage. We can hide our anger or choose to express it openly. It can be a destructive emotion when it seeks to hurt someone else, breed unforgiveness, or extol revenge. Gary Collins wrote, "Anger, openly expressed, deliberately hidden from others or unconsciously expressed, is at the basis of a host of psychological, physical and spiritual problems. Behind most hot tempers and overstressed lives is a root of fear. It could be fear of not getting the promotion we desire, fear of being hurt on the expressway, fear of not being able to handle the next challenge in front of us, or fear of not getting to an important meeting on time. Whenever we are presented with a situation that scares us, if we see no way out, we pull out our last primitive defense—we get mad.

Like a dog trapped in a corner, we growl, rear up, and snarl in order to scare away our attackers. When we become this threatened, we tend to lose our capacity for reason. As Robert Green Ingersoll described it, "Anger blows out the lamp of the mind."

When anger is rooted in fear, we automatically focus all our energy on our perceived need to protect ourselves; this blinds us from seeing how we are acting aggressively to those around us. Whenever we feel threatened, whatever the cause, our natural inclination will be to feel hurt, forcing us to put up our walls of defense. Consequently, all of our attention goes to caring for our need to protect our interests. We automatically become less concerned with others and their well-being. Whenever we embrace our fears, protect our own interests, and become angry, we render ourselves incapable of embracing those around us.

Anger's—and Fear's—Intensity

The intensity of our anger is always proportionate to the depth of our fears and the intensity of our needs. No matter what the issue is—food, love, shelter, or finances—when we fear that our needs will not be met, our anxiety levels rise, causing us to convert those fearful feelings to anger. This conversion process is as predictable as the stars coming out every night.

When our core needs of safety and security are not met, we become afraid that they will never be met. We try to control the world around us in order to insure there will be a response to our needs. The longer our needs go unmet, the more afraid and controlling we become. If our requests, tactics, or manipulations do not result in our needs being met, our fears grow. As our fears grow, we then empower them with greater anger and control.

This "fear to anger" paradigm is often played out in relationships where our need to be loved is unmet. For some of us, when our needs in a significant relationship are not met, our immediate response is to register some degree of anger with the person we perceive is withholding love. We empower our fear of not getting our needs met by expressing some level of irritation. As a result, the fundamental role anger plays in our lives is to be a protector and defender of our unfulfilled desires, unmet needs, and fears.

Understanding the Fear-Anger-Control Loop

We know when two live wires make contact, sparks fly. We know when a cold front and warm front meet, the likelihood of thunderstorms increases. The same probable conditions for volatility also exist in relationships. Whenever two people hold a conversation, the chances are they will, over time, enter into various levels and intensities of conflict. Differences are inevitable in relationships. Living a healthy and productive life requires us to manage our fears and anger by learning how to share our needs and desires openly and nondefensively.

The process of resolving the problems in our lives can cause many people to develop their own interactive dance. Whether husband and wife, father and daughter, boss and employee, or some other pair, their tribal dances usually display what we call a loop. A relational loop occurs when one person brings his or her differing value sets and ways of viewing the world into the communication process. Like a dog chasing a cat in a circle, relational loops occur when one person's actions trigger the other person to respond in a particular way.

When someone supercharges his fears with anger and moves into a loop, he generally does so more with those he knows and values the most. With his acquaintances, he generally restrains himself from unleashing his deepest needs or fear of being rejected.

Every married couple we have counseled over the years has experienced to one degree or another the fear-anger-control loop. I (Ray) witnessed the loop in action vividly one session when Sandra and Joel entered the office. Sandra was ready to explode shortly into our session. She explained that Joel had gambled away his paycheck again. Their financial situation was unstable at best. It was increasingly difficult to pay the bills at the end of the month with four children to feed and clothe.

As Sandra talked, Joel began to stiffen in his chair. I asked for his reaction to his wife's complaints.

"This is what I deal with at home. She gets so controlling and angry. That's why I stay away. I have more fun with the guys than I do with her."

"How is staying away from home and having fun with the guys helping the family?"

Joel became uneasy and hung his head. He then quietly said, "It's not."

I gently looked at him and asked him what his behavior was saying about his needs. Joel replied, "I have a lot of pressure at work. I try to get as much overtime as I can because I know we need the money to cover the bills. But sometimes the pressure at work and home gets too much and I have to blow off steam somewhere, so I go to the casino with the guys."

I turned to Sandra and asked if she had ever heard her husband express his feelings in this way. "I don't think I ever heard Joel share his feelings like that before," Sandra replied. Her facial expression had softened and her tone of voice was saying "I would like to hear more of his true feelings."

Time after time we have watched hearts soften when the two "dancers" disclose their real needs and express their feelings. Every person longs to have someone with whom he or she can honestly share and from whom he or she can receive comfort for their hurts.

When those in the fear-anger-control loop finally reach the core of their pain, they realize the need to change. When I further explained to Sandra and Joel the dynamics of their loop, they began to recognize the real reasons for their behavior and attitudes.

As Joel and I discussed the reasons behind his gambling, he opened up further. He felt like a failure because he wasn't able to earn more money for his family. He explained, "I feel so ashamed. Isn't a guy supposed to provide for his family?" Joel went on to say, "When Sandra gets angry and controlling, I feel so criticized by her, which only makes me feel more alone and even more like a failure."

Soon Joel began to realize that his addiction to gambling was his way to medicate the painful fear of being a failure and to avoid facing the terrible hurt of his wife's rejection. He further admitted that his anger was his way to keep her at bay so she would leave him alone and not remind him of his failures.

While Joel was making all these discoveries and connections, Sandra was able to see the goodwill and warm heart of her husband. As she saw Joel's openness in admitting his needs and feelings, Sandra began to admit her own controlling behavior.

In a spirit of openness and reflection, Sandra said, "The reason I would sometimes get controlling is that sometimes I was afraid that our children would not be taken care of in the ways they needed. You see, one of our children has a disability which regularly taps our savings account. When Joel retreats and doesn't respond to my fears, I get angry."

Joel piped up and said, "That's why I distance myself."

"And Joel, when you do that," Sandra noted, "I feel abandoned and left with all the pressure."

Over time they both learned how to share their feelings openly and honestly, without accusation and judgment. Gradually they began to change some of their lifelong patterns. Becoming good managers of fear demands our willingness to identify and express our fears openly before converting them to angry responses. Insight into our own behavior always precedes the ability to take action and the opportunity to see real change.

Defusing Fear's Power

Whenever we clearly identify our fears, we defuse their power over us. As we have noted, it takes courage to face our fears. Both Sandra and Joel faced their fears by identifying what and why they were afraid. As Sandra identified her fear that Joel was not wanting to provide for the family, she was able to see Joel communicate the actual opposite of her fear: Joel was so concerned about his ability to provide that he thought of little else. Joel in turn was able to express his fear that Sandra didn't believe in him. He too realized that his fears were ungrounded. Sandra was supportive of him, but she was allowing her fear to cloud her reactions to Joel.

As they shared their fears, they were able to hear each other's real feelings for the first time. This laid the groundwork for each of them to support each other rather than create another conflict that would only serve to distance them more.

Expressing Our Anger in Wrong Ways

We all deal with anger in unique ways. Some of us lash out at others when we convert our fear to anger; others internalize feelings, expressing their anger in more subtle ways.

We have identified three common unhealthy ways we express our anger when fueled by fear. They are: (1) censoring our anger, (2) becoming combative with our anger, and (3) being cunning with our anger.

1. Censoring Our Anger

When we censor or repress anger, we automatically bury our feelings alive. Driven deep underground, this anger begins to fester, poisoning our souls. At that point, our ability to identify the root causes of our anger is all but eliminated. When we censor our feelings, we render ourselves incapable of identifying what we are really feeling.

We expend 70 percent of our emotional energy when we repress our sadness, anger, fear, and hurt, says psychiatrist Fritz Perls. To censor these emotions is to cut off our human vitality. When we continue to hold in our feelings, we automatically throw off our emotional equilibrium. We begin the slow process of hardening our hearts.

Maybe you have met someone who has become emotionally cold. He or she may say things like, "Only weak people show their feelings." The person doesn't see the value in feelings at all. His or her defense against feeling anything, particularly more dynamic emotions like fear and anger, is to appear that nothing has fazed them at all. The individual appears to be fully in control. By censoring feelings of anger/fear, he then feels no obligation to deal with these feelings at all.

Adults may censor personal anger for many reasons. One common reason is that they saw anger censored in their families as children. The strong message in some families was that anger is destructive and should never be expressed. On the other hand, some anger-censors might have been raised in families where they saw a great deal of anger expressed in destructive ways; in response, they resolved that they would contain angry feelings when they arose.

Many people who repress their feelings of anger may believe that they do not have the right to be angry. They may see themselves as less than caring, loving people if they do get angry. They may also believe that if they do get angry, it will hurt the other person, and conclude it is better to repress the feeling.

Anger left unattended will turn to bitterness. In the end, repression not only leads to bitterness, but health-related disorders and fragmented relationships with God and others. In addition, anger repressed over time can move into depression and/or anxiety.

The following checklist will help you identify if you have a tendency to repress your feelings when you become angry.

❑ I am very image conscious.

❑ I tend to be a private person.

❑ Under all conditions I like to appear that I have it "together."

❑ I feel problems take care of themselves without having to discuss it.

❑ I sometimes can harbor a grudge.

❑ I suffer from stress-related ailments (such as headaches, stomach acid).

❑ I tend to avoid situations in which strong emotion is being expressed.

❑ I see nothing good coming from the intense expression of emotion.

❑ I become easily overwhelmed by stressful situations.

❑ I struggle with bouts of depression and/or anxiety.

2. Becoming Combative with Our Anger

Do you see your anger as a weapon? Those who become combative often feel that they have no alternative but to show their frustrations. You may be unknowingly saying, "I am afraid right now and I don't know how to control the situation." You then may force your feelings onto others. We can do this in several ways: lashing out, yelling, intimidating, blaming, and/or criticizing others.

Some of us may see expressing anger as a way to show

strength and power in the situation at hand and a way to compensate for our feelings of inferiority. This is often called the "peacocking effect." Like a peacock that spreads its wings to its full span to scare off its attackers, we come on strong with our anger in order to get those who threaten us to back away. It can also have the effect of keeping those around us emotionally distant so we are not threatened by having to get emotionally close. Pride controllers and power controllers, as discussed in chapter 8, will often show their anger more aggressively.

Many times, we are openly combative at the expense of another person. We demand that others consider us and meet our need, yet we may not be aware of how intensely we are coming across. When a baseball pitcher reaches back for a little more power on a fastball and then hits the batter, his need for speed overrides his ability to be accurate. Likewise, when we are aggressive with our anger, our immediate needs may get met, but in the end we sacrifice the quality of the relationship. We also risk physically harming others and compromising our own physical and mental health as well.

To further assist you in identifying if you might be combative with your anger, we have provided the following checklist.

❑ I like to "say it the way it is" and if others don't like it, it is their problem.

❑ My voice becomes increasingly louder when I am in the midst of a disagreement.

❑ I feel it is important for others to see my point of view.

❑ I have a tendency to be tenacious about others agreeing with me.

❑ When something goes wrong, I focus so sharply on fixing the problem that I overlook other people's feelings.

❏ I tend to see arguments as something to be won or lost.

❏ I can be forceful and harsh in my disagreements with others.

❏ I tend to be the first to express my opinion.

❏ I can be strong-willed.

3. Being Cunning with Our Anger

A third unhealthy way we can express our anger is by using cunning, which involves the least amount of risk for us personally. Our anger is expressed but in an indirect way; so a husband who is frustrated with his wife's nagging him to take out the garbage will repeatedly "forget" to take the garbage out when he is supposed to. He then sees his wife's frustration and feels a momentary release of his own angry feelings.

People who are cunning in their expression of anger generally feel a lack of confidence in their ability to express their anger in a direct manner. Consequently, their anger will surface in ways which are difficult for others to readily identify.

Those who use cunning expressions fear failure and rejection from others so keenly that they retreat from any hint of strong emotion. That is why they tend to operate more in secrecy than in open expression—they fear their ideas and feelings will be rejected. The expression, "I don't get mad; I get even" could be the bumper sticker for those of us who are cunning in expressing our anger. Passive controllers often express their anger in these types of ways.

Those of us who are cunning will have a tendency toward procrastination or lateness as a way to make a statement to those with whom we feel threatened or angry. When we are late we are saying, "I don't like you telling me what to do, so I will let you know by my actions who is really in charge."

Rather than openly expressing our anger, we hold grudges

and indirectly punish the person with whom we are angry. We feel if we are honest, it would mean we might jeopardize our ability to gain and maintain the upper hand. The following is a checklist to evaluate if this may be your style.

- ❏ I am prone to pouting to get my way.
- ❏ When I get angry, I withdraw from others as a way to frustrate them.
- ❏ I have a tendency to procrastinate—especially things I do not enjoy doing.
- ❏ When I am angry, I will pretend that everything is fine when it is not.
- ❏ I prefer to be left alone.
- ❏ When someone talks to me about my problems, I dig in my heels and become resistant.
- ❏ I sometimes do things to get others angry.
- ❏ I am easily intimidated by those who are angry.
- ❏ I have a tendency to be forgetful.
- ❏ I feel powerless in disagreements with others.

What Are We to Do?

There have been conflicting views as to how to deal with anger. Some researchers believe that it is best that we express our feelings of anger with intensity—whatever that intensity might be. Such expression allows us to think more clearly about what causes us to be angry, they argue. Other researchers believe giving full vent to our anger only makes things worse by complicating an already bad situation.

In addition, expressing anger can magnify the angry feelings we already have. Researcher Ebbe Ebbesen did a study of engineers and technicians who were experiencing frustration after being recently fired by an aerospace company. Some of the former employees were asked questions that offered the opportunity to openly release hostility, such as "What instances can you think of where the company has not been fair with you?" When these people later filled out a questionnaire that assessed their attitudes toward the company, compared with those who had not been given the freedom to vent their anger, those who had let out their feelings without restraint were more hostile toward the company overall.[3]

This study confirmed findings from a 1999 study conducted by the American Psychological Association. Acting out our anger freely actually increases it. Individuals who hit punching bags or other objects actually escalate their feelings of aggression.

Although we may feel temporary relief once we have expressed ourselves, the angry feeling can be reinforcing and habit-forming. Each time we become angry, we will tend to react to the intensity of anger that we previously experienced. A coach who loses his temper at his basketball players for the first time will be more likely to immediately lash out at them with the same intensity when presented with a similar situation.

Therefore we recommend not denying the emotion of anger but identifying what has caused (fueled) your anger. Is it unmet needs or unrealized expectations? To express anger without any identification of what is causing us to become angry only leaves us wanting to go ballistic. On the other hand, when we work at identifying the causes of our anger, we begin the process of working toward dissipating our anger by gaining insights as to what our unmet needs, unfulfilled desires, and fears are. That process affords us the opportunity to move toward learning how to communicate our needs and to move closer to forgiving those who have hurt us.

We can become angry for various reasons. In this chapter we have focused on anger that is related to not facing our fears. Let's look at specific steps to deal with this powerful emotion.

First, acknowledge your feelings of anger. Recognize that feeling anger is as natural as feeling sad or happy; it is how you express anger that makes all the difference.

Second, give yourself emotional distance from the situation. Remember the old adage of counting to ten. When you take time out from the situation that has prompted your anger, you give your body the time to calm down from the adrenaline that is pumped through your system when you are angry. When your physiological arousal is calmed, you are less apt to act impulsively and are able to think rationally.

Third, reflect on what you are afraid of. Ask yourself the following questions:

1. Am I perceiving the situation accurately?
2. Am I creating anxiety over something that is not evident?
3. Am I distorting the situation by exaggerating the possible outcome?
4. What major fears—failure, rejection, abandonment, death—might I be experiencing right now?
5. Are my fears related to feeling inferior and wanting to compensate for those feelings?
6. Am I afraid of my rights being violated?

Fourth, ask yourself what you really need.

1. Clarify in your own mind if what you are wanting is really a need or a desire.

2. Be aware that historical unmet needs will always intensify how we express our need to people on a daily basis. For example, when someone is not listening to us the intensity of our reaction might be due in part that we came from a home where our mother/father was emotionally distant and not interested in hearing our thoughts and feelings.

3. Needs are not right or wrong in themselves. It is how we express these needs that can become appropriate or not.

4. When you ask for what you need, be open to accept what you get.

Fifth, remind yourself of four key facts:

1. You can only change yourself. You cannot change those around you or the circumstances.

2. Others deserve the benefit of the doubt. Unless you are shown otherwise, assume the best motives of another. When shown otherwise, remember that you can be thoughtless also. We are all fallible and human.

3. Your anger hurts you more than it hurts others. It affects your peace of mind, your relationships, and body.

4. The issue may not be worth the tension. Ask yourself the question: In the big picture, is this issue worth the stress?

Sixth, watch for emotional payoffs. We react in certain ways because there is a benefit to us, even though it might appear destructive. Ask yourself what you might gain from being angry. Is it being able to be in a position of dominance in a relationship? Is it a temporary feeling of being in control? Does it provide a distraction from the real issue of your own personal growth?

Seventh, determine a course of action. Do you need to speak with the person that offended you? How can you specifically change the situation that provokes you?

Eighth, follow the slogan from the recovery movement: "Let go and let God." Release what you cannot control to the One who holds you, and trust God for the outcome.

Anger can be directed toward a healthy end when we are in charge of it. Anger can motivate us to take appropriate action. The energy that we feel when we are angry can be fueled to a constructive end. We can become more productive in problem-solving alternative solutions. We don't need to resort to censoring, being combative, or being cunning with our anger. When we have mastered the fears that fuel our anger, not only we but others will benefit from it as well.

CHAPTER TEN

When Love Heals Our Hurts

*No one can make you feel inferior
without your consent.*

❖

ELEANOR ROOSEVELT

People will hurt us. In relationships pain is inevitable. That harsh reality makes having relationships fearful, knowing that someone may wound us or we may wound someone else.

From unintentional insensitivities to malicious words intended to deeply wound, we all have experienced hurt. When we are wounded we have a tendency to withdraw or retaliate. A central theme of *From Fear to Love* has been that when we are afraid, we will try to control those around us in order to get our needs met. When those needs still are not met to our satisfaction, we supercharge our fears with anger and control more intensely. When we fuel our fear-anger-control dynamic, we affect our ability to love others. Hurting someone becomes the inevitable consequence when we try to control them with our anger fueled by our fears. We all know how it feels to have a scraped knee, cut finger, or a torn muscle, but none of these physical hurts can be as painful as a broken heart. Yet every person at one time or another has hurt or been hurt by someone they love. The hurts that wound our hearts center on our unmet needs for love and acceptance.

Sadness and Anger Together

The emotion of hurt is defined as feeling sadness and anger at the same time. When we have been hurt, we feel as though a ton of bricks has been dumped on our chests. Often our shoulders and heads actually droop, and we feel like we want to cry and hit somebody at the same time. When we begin to think about our hurts, we start to realize that we have felt rejected by someone we care about or an important need has not been met. When we experience rejection, our hopes are dashed that we can get our needs met in the relationship, and our fears rise to the surface.

To be hurt is like walking in the mud with our boots on. We are unable to move freely because the mud keeps holding us back. Over time, those collective hurts make us feel we are emotionally stuck in the mud, wondering if we will have the energy to overcome the negative feelings of anger and sadness.

Needs, Desires, and Pain

Our needs refer to that which sustains life—either spiritually, emotionally, physically, or mentally. Our desires refer to how these needs can be met. For example, our bodies need protein to function properly, while the type of protein we might prefer refers to our desires. We all need protein, but we don't necessarily need steak and lobster as our source of protein.

The challenge we all face is how to get our needs met in

healthy and desirable ways. Due to the unique nature of our needs, there are always expectations attached to them.

The lack of fulfillment of those expectations is what causes all of us to get angry on a variety of levels.

As therapists, we consistently see how people project their hurts onto others and how this is directly related to needs and desires on some level not being met. When we take time to listen to the words of others who have experienced significant emotional pain, they inevitably describe the pain they felt when someone either in silence or rudeness said no to their requests. Hundreds of individuals over the years have told us their stories of not having a mother, father, husband, wife, or significant other love them when they needed it the most.

The collective hurts that people carry can turn into a ball and chain. The length of that chain always corresponds to the number of hurts that they have chosen to hang on to. For some, the chain has become so heavy and long that they have become emotionally crippled. In a real sense, they have chosen to nurse their hurts rather than reach out for help and take responsibility for their pain.

Pain That Motivates

Yet hurt can play a redemptive role in our lives if we allow it. Pain can motivate us to examine our hearts to see how we are living in ways that are not helpful for ourselves or others. It can motivate us to make changes which can make our life more meaningful and productive. It can lead us to forgive, risk, trust, and be more honest in relationships.

When Cheryl and Edward came to Nancy for counseling, they were two steps away from calling their thirty-two-year marriage quits. Our initial session revealed that the years of hurt had created an icy wall of silence between them. As they recalled some of their most painful moments with each other, it was as if the experiences had happened yesterday. Cheryl recalled comments that Edward had made on their honeymoon. Edward remembered telling Cheryl about experiences in his first job, only to find his wife wholly uninterested.

It is not unusual to see people keep their hurt alive by constantly rehearsing in their mind old experiences. For Cheryl and Edward, the hurt finally became a catalyst to seeing how they had kept their marriage from moving forward. They had placed most of their emotional energy into blaming each other for the years of heartache.

We have stated that life is pain management. Understandably, much of our emotional pain comes from our hurts. Learning how to manage our hurts takes time, energy, and a focus that says, "I want to learn the skills necessary that will enable me to put my hurts to rest rather than bury them alive." When someone has buried their hurts alive, those unresolved hurts will always drive and motivate us to react in ways that become habits of responding. A key principle is that we hurt others in response to being hurt. The hurts of our past often become the unconscious copilot in our lives. The only way to remove their influence is by becoming aware of how your hurts are influencing your life in a negative way.

Motivated to Recognize Hurts

A key tool that allows us to unhook ourselves from the past so we can move freely into the present moment is to recognize how past hurts are influencing our lives. This is how we become able to love free of the influence of hurt.

Cheryl and Edward needed to move beyond their feelings to find insights into how their marriage became so painful. They needed to evaluate how much they wanted to see their marriage restored. They needed to make a commitment to be willing to look more closely at their own contribution to the difficulties in their marriage. They needed to begin to let go of the hurts of the past and resolve to begin anew.

Motivated to Change

When we feel hurt, it can also help us to make changes we would not normally have made.

Andrew worked in his family's business while Amy went to school and managed all the household duties. When they came to Ray for counseling, Amy began by saying, "We just can't discuss anything of importance without getting into a fight." Andrew chimed in and said, "Whenever I bring up a concern, she seems to be more interested in being with her friends and volunteering her time than being at home. Whenever I bring this up, she goes ballistic!"

As they continued telling their story, it quickly became evident that they had both felt rejected by each from the very start of their marriage. Their hurt feelings were piling up.

At one point Amy said, "I'd be more willing to stay at home if he would stop being so critical and quit seeing the world so negatively."

Ray asked Andrew what he thought about Amy's comments. "I can always anticipate that she will nag me for not seeing things her way," he said, "so I just keep myself busy with my job and spend time with my friends."

Asked what it felt like to hear what the other was saying, each responded by commenting that they felt hurt by the actions and attitudes of the other.

As they explored the source of their hurt, they both realized areas in which they needed to change. Andrew needed to work on his tendency to see the world through dark lenses and avoid Amy rather than sharing honestly his feelings. Amy realized that her nagging was actually distancing Andrew and not accomplishing anything productive. The hurt in their relationship became a positive catalyst to make changes they may not necessarily have been willing to make.

The Influence of Our Growing Years

Most of us haven't had modeled for us positive ways of dealing with our hurts. As children and teens, we may have watched a parent (or even brother or sister) respond to hurt by blaming someone, or by throwing an emotional temper tantrum in hopes of trying to make everyone dance to his or her tune. At other times, we may have watched a family member respond by either going ballistic or withdrawing into a depression. No matter what someone's personal style or personality expression of dealing with hurt is, we are all forced at some point to react to those hurts that have not been resolved in our lives.

Ray recalls a conversation with a friend we'll call Dan in which Ray took a risk and talked vulnerably about a stressful situation. Dan responded warmly and empathetically. Weeks passed, yet Dan never followed up on the conversation. He acted as if Ray had never shared anything with him. Ray became hurt that Dan appeared to not be genuinely interested in Ray's difficult time. Mixed in with the hurt was anger and sadness—anger that his expectations of the friendship had not been met and sadness of losing the opportunity to realize genuine support in a difficult time. It appeared Dan just didn't seem to care enough to follow up.

Ray reflected, prayed, and waited for the right time to talk with Dan. Hearing Ray's concern, Dan acknowledged that he didn't follow up as a friend should. As the discussion continued, he said, "Look, Ray, I felt honored by your vulnerability.

But it also threatened me. I wasn't sure I wanted to be in relationships that demand that I be vulnerable also. I'm still not. You pursued our getting together, not me."

As Ray's friend shared these things, Ray realized that he had buried some hurts centered around his own dad. Ray realized that the avoiding, self-absorbed nature of his dad's alcoholic patterns taught Ray to be the pursuer in relationships. As a young boy, Ray learned that if he didn't pursue his dad he wouldn't get anything from him. Ray's persistence with his dad was his only way to maintain hope that he might one day connect with him.

In the process, Ray in effect burned out his internal sensor that would say, "You are putting more energy into the relationship than he is." The lack of ability to sense and evaluate the disproportionate nature of his relationship with his dad carried over to his relationship with Dan. Like most of us, his growing-up years affected his responses as an adult.

By making these emotional and intellectual connections, Ray has been able to freely evaluate his current relationships. Ray now applies what he calls the "equal energy" principle. Now he measures the energy someone is willing to make in relationship and decides to equal that energy. That is not to say that Ray doesn't, at times, choose to be the initiator; it means that he more wisely initiates and matches the energy of the person he is building a relationship with.

You can see how the hurts of our past can become copilots in our lives. The only way to remove those copilots is by becoming aware of how they are influencing our lives in negative ways. These insights become one of the power tools that allow us to unhook ourselves from the past in order to move more freely into the future unobstructed and able to love without strings attached.

How to Let Our Hurts Go

The goal: to become unchained from our hurts as well as have the skills to manage them. When this happens, we can keep a short account with our hurts; in turn, we become and are freed up to reach out and help—and hug—others.

Feeling Safe and Secure with People

Some very important conditions must be met in order for us to be honest with others when we are feeling hurt. First, we must feel safe with the person we are wanting to share our feelings with. When you can risk sharing your hurts and still feel safe, you will then move to the next level—being able to trust that person with your deeper feelings. As your trust grows, you will naturally risk more in hopes that you will continue to feel safe and secure. This will automatically open the door to becoming vulnerable with sharing your hurts and coming closer to those you trust. Safety, security, risk, trust, and honesty are the key elements to being able to share, process, and resolve emotional pain.

Choosing to Have a Servant's Heart

Each one of us could tell a story of how we have been hurt by another person. When we choose to adopt a loving servant heart, we dramatically affect how we will enter into the process of helping to heal one another's hurts. To keep from letting others hurt you, be willing to take the initiative in the relationship, setting the right tone. The tone should encourage, not discourage, the process of sharing and resolving those hurts in the relationship.

The key element to successfully resolve those hurts between two people is to set up an atmosphere in which both feel safe and secure. When you both feel safe, your willingness to risk entering into a conversation about your hurtful feelings or experience will be enhanced. And with such feelings of being safe, we will find ourselves growing in our trust that what we have to say and how we feel will not be rejected. As safety and security continue to grow, our risk grows, our trust increases; and we begin to go deeper in our willingness to be more honest with our thoughts and feelings.

When someone has hurt you, how do you move from feelings of hurt to restoration and renewed trust? We recommend these steps:

1. Take responsibility for your feelings of hurt.

2. Gain awareness into the nature of your hurt feelings. Check out the historical nature of your hurt. When your reaction is more intense than the situation warrants, it's a sign that historical feelings are coming to the surface. What are they?

3. Identify what you are angry about. (The feeling of hurt is generally a combination of sadness and anger.) What expectations do you have? What have you lost in the relationship—trust . . . respect?

4. Communicate specifically the behavior and/or statements that offended you.

5. Check out with the other person if he or she understands what has hurt you and how it affected you.

6. Invite the person to take ownership of his or her hurtful attitudes and behaviors.

7. Receive the person's apology.

8. Personally make the choice to forgive the individual. Know that forgiveness takes time and a diligent effort to let go of the pain that someone else has inflicted.

Relationships that have endured the stormy times and have come through to the other side of healing and forgiveness have a new depth of love. Not only is a new depth of love achieved, but a greater level of commitment is also experienced.

Love That
Overcomes

And the end of all our exploring
Will be to arrive where we started
And know the place for the first time.

T. S. ELIOT
"THE FOUR QUARTETS"

We began this book chronicling what happens when you and I are gripped by fear. Ray and I fought fear in our eleven-year wilderness experience. This book has looked at how fear powerfully shapes the direction of American culture. We've also looked at how we deal with fear individually. Particularly in chapters 4–6 and 8 we saw the relational fears that drive us and the controlling behaviors we adopt when we fear our needs will not be met. We discussed how, when our controlling behavior doesn't satisfy our needs for safety, we become angry (chapter 9). Finally, we learned that the antidote to the insidious effect of fear is love—a love that not only honors and cares for others but ourselves as well.

We have now come full circle. We look once more at our society, but this time let's catch a vision for what it looks like when love is put into action. What would happen in our communities if we chose to move beyond the oppressive burden of fear and make deliberate choices to care for and love others?

The answer is: We *can* be agents of change to make our culture better. We can affect each other for the greater good. We don't have to be victims of the cultural tides. As the old adage states, "The only thing for evil to reign supreme is for good men to do nothing." It is up to each one of us to make our communities places where love and respect are part of our daily life. It is up to us to undo the terrible effects of hatred, poverty, and disease. Like pouring water into a glass until it overflows, when we are filled with love we can't help but spill out care and compassion around us. We are then able to stand up against the strong tides of turmoil, prejudice, irrationality, and isolation in our society.

Love Turns Turmoil into Acts of Bravery

On September 11, 2001, the lives of all Americans changed forever. The cruel attack on New York City's World Trade Center and the Pentagon could have brought us to our knees in terror; instead, it became evidence of our collective, inherent courage. Since that horrible day there have been literally thousands of individual acts of bravery testifying to a renewing sense of community in our country.

All of us carry images of courage and love in our memories from that fateful day. Firefighters charging up the stairs of the World Trade Center as office workers frantically streamed down the stairs to safety. Some remember the selfless love of Chaplain Mychal Judge, who was killed while administering last rites to the initial victims of the attacks. Others recall the courage of flight attendant Madeline Amy Sweeney, who called her supervisor on the ground and provided a coolheaded account of the hijacking of American Airlines Flight 11, first alerting authorities to the attack. Most know about the extraordinary heroism of five passengers aboard Flight 93: Todd Beamer, Mark Bingham, Tom Burnett, Jeremy Glick, and Lou Nacke, who banded together in the final minutes of their lives to rush the cockpit. Their struggle to overcome the hijackers brought the plane to earth and, from most accounts, saved a national monument from attack and more loss of life.[1]

Instead of fear, we saw repeated responses of love and gratitude. Firehouses were decked with flowers and swarming with people wanting to make donations for the families of those who had loved ones die. People lined up throughout the city to donate blood. And countless others—from rescue workers to police officers to health care workers to ordinary citizens—gave in ways that seemed humanly impossible.

When fear grips us, we have a choice. We can either withdraw into ourselves or tap into our personal courage. We can change our fear into love. In the waning months of 2001 in New York and across America, we saw love chase fear. Like beacons of light, certain individuals illumined a path for us to follow. They have showed us that when love and courage prevail, anything can be overcome.

Love Turns Isolation into a Sense of Belonging

Through Compassion

When we care for those in need, we tenderly go about meeting their needs in any way we can. Compassionate people go beyond identifying the needs and willingly sacrifice their own personal comfort for the sake of those grieving with heartache or exploding with anxiety. When we show compassion, we are willing to let go of our own need for security and safety to help others. We in turn become "safe places" for those who are in need of refuge.

Such compassion identifies with the pain of the hurting. As one writer describes it,

> Compassion is not a snob gone slumming. Anyone can salve his conscience by an occasional foray into knitting for the (handicapped). Did you ever take a real trip down inside the broken heart of a friend? To feel the sob of the soul—the raw, red crucible of emotional agony? To have this become almost as much yours as that of your soul-crushed neighbor? Then, to sit down with him—and silently weep? This is the beginning of compassion.[2]

Through Sacrifice for Others

Mother Teresa was an individual who loved the "soul-crushed neighbor" by sacrificing her personal welfare to care for the dying in the streets of Calcutta, India. Not only did she sacrifice her own well-being, she courageously faced cultural and religious barriers to meet those in great poverty.

Whenever she and her sisters in the Missionaries of Charity found people cast off and dying in the streets and garbage dumps, they brought them to her hospital and cared for them tenderly and graciously. These people were clearly victims of extreme physical poverty. Mother Teresa, however, believed that the greatest poverty is not the lack of food but the poverty of the heart—to be unwanted and unloved. Mother Teresa and her sisters ministered to not only the physical needs but to the needs of the heart. She and her sisters provided a place of belonging and comfort to those cast out by society. The lepers, the neglected, the unwanted, and the dying all found love and care from Mother Teresa and her Missionaries of Charity.

In 1979 Mother Teresa received the Nobel Peace Prize. Unlike most peace prize winners, the peace she sought was not political but spiritual. Mother Teresa has said, "Our work is not our vocation, our vocation is to love Christ." When she cared for the brokenhearted and dying, she loved them as if she were loving Christ Himself.

Mother Teresa believed that giving is a mutual thing in relationships. Those we care for become our teachers in a very real sense. "I will never forget one day in Venezuela," she wrote, "when I went to visit a family who had given us a lamb. I went to thank them and there I found out that they had a badly crippled child. I asked the mother, 'What is the child's name?' The mother gave me a most beautiful answer. 'We call him "Teacher of Love" because he keeps on teaching us how to love. Everything we do for him is our love for God in action.'"[3]

Mother Teresa died September 5, 1997. A week later her funeral became one of the most moving in history. An incredible cross section of people gathered, from the well-known to the little-known, from people from countries around the world to people from the streets of Calcutta. Those who participated in the service represented well those whom Mother Teresa loved: A leper whose nose was half gone and face withered offered a chalice of wine; a little orphan girl carried a basket of flowers; and a handicapped boy smiled as he struggled to walk up to the altar with the bread.[4] Each represented Mother Teresa's mission to love the "poorest of poor" regardless of their status or pain.

Love Turns Irrational Fears into Acts of Service

When we meet someone for the first time, we generally draw conclusions on what we see and who he or she is. For example, a woman with a history of abuse from men may meet a newly hired assertive male colleague and immediately assume that he is like all the other men who have harmed her. A man who has experienced racial hatred may be fearful of working for a boss of a different color. But to love as God has called us to love is to go beyond our initial perceptions and see into the very heart of others. To love as God has called us to love is to set aside our preconceived notions in order to enter into another's life and know them in all their uniqueness. Such love leads to gracious acts of service.

This accepting and giving love occurs when we refuse to stereotype others; then we are not limited by one's race, position, or economic status. We are free to see the character, value, and worth of others as people made in the image of God. When we suspend our judgments and conclusions, we no longer see people as good or bad, successful or failing, acceptable or unacceptable. We then realize that all they ever really want (like us) is to be loved.

Jean Vanier has inspired many to reconsider their irrational judgments and assumptions and live a life characterized by love. After a career in the navy, achieving a doctorate in philosophy, and a college teaching career, Vanier began a humble vocation of caring full time for two mentally handicapped men, Raphael and Phillippe, in Trosly-Breuil, France. This ministry quickly developed into a community called L'Arche, which included residential housing and programs for the severely mentally impaired.

Today L'Arche has grown to 103 communities in 27 countries. In each residential community, members with diverse backgrounds live together with no distinction made because of race, religious tradition, or social class. Most L'Arche residents have come from state institutions where they have had little contact with their own families. Some of the residents have spent their entire lives being moved from one institution to another. L'Arche becomes for them a permanent home and sanctuary.

These communities feature homes where intellectually disabled adults and their nonhandicapped assistants live together as family and friends. For many of the mentally disabled residents, L'Arche is their first genuine encounter in an environment where family, friends, and relationships have real meaning. Vanier's goal is to provide a place where everyone realizes a degree of dignity and happiness that would not be found in an institution.

Sadly, of course, many societies, including our American society, typecast mentally handicapped adults as having nothing to offer and being a burden on society. Many feel apprehensive in relating to them because mentally handicapped people communicate in their own unique way. Yet Vanier has exposed this fear as irrational, helping people throughout the world see that mentally handicapped adults are people who are dearly loved and valued by God. He rightly argues that they can teach us much about the nature of unconditional love through their childlike acceptance of those around them. Vanier and his team are able to see beyond the physical limitations of the disabilities of the handicapped to the beauty of their hearts inside.

"You see," Vanier explains, "people with mental disabilities have been pushed aside, they've been seen as no good, as being a problem, as being a dramatic effect inside of a family . . . what we discover is that they have a heart, that they're simple, they're loving."

On the web site for the L'Arche community in Canada, one story typifies the simple joy that occurs in these communities. "One night Pat, the director of the community, during a time of prayer and reflection asked the residents, 'In our reading, the word love appears three times. Can anyone tell me what love is?' There was silence, then Dovie, a core member, answered, 'Sure. Love is when God holds you tight.'"[5]

185

Vanier has given his life to a profound and meaningful call-ing: caring for the disadvantaged, the lonely, and the dispossessed. He has been willing to devote his life to love those whom we may regard as difficult to relate to, time-consuming, and unpro-ductive. He has shown the world that mentally handicapped adults teach us what is most important in life—a caring touch and understanding. Vanier shows us the power that love has to bring dignity and happiness to the unwanted and neglected, who can now realize their value and worth as individuals. Vanier and his workers point us to a profound yet simple truth: Everyone has worth and is loved of God, deserving of our love.

Love Helps Us to Pray for Our Enemies

"Love your enemies and pray for those who persecute you," Jesus said (Matthew 5:44). There is great wisdom in this. In this world we will always encounter evil. The very nature of evil is to destroy, intimidate, and immobilize us. But, when we love, we show our enemies that good can overcome evil. We show those who seek to harm us that their evil behavior and intentions do not have power over us. And as we have noted throughout this book in true-life examples, "Perfect love drives out fear" (1 John 4:18).

Ruby Nell Bridges modeled this principle as a tenderhearted six-year-old. Her story is retold by sociologist Robert Coles of Harvard University. On November 14, 1960, Ruby Bridges con-fidently stepped into William Frantz Elementary School, one of only four African-American students to integrate New Orleans schools—and the only African-American at Frantz Ele-mentary. Six years earlier the U. S. Supreme Court had made the landmark decision ordering the desegregation of all schools (in Brown vs. the Board of Education).

The nation watched the nightly newscasts showing federal

marshals escorting her into the school building. But except for her teacher, Ruby's classroom was empty. Parents refused to let their children be with Ruby; for months, Ruby was the only student with her teacher. During her first day and for some time afterward, the unrelenting crowds, including abusive and taunting adults, bombarded Ruby as she entered and left the school. One woman continually threatened to poison her. Of all the comments hurled at her, this one woman's harassment brought such anxiety to Ruby that it became difficult for her to eat meals with her family for fear that she would actually be poisoned.

Ruby's daily journey to school each day took her past threatening mobs hurling insults and messages of hate. One morning, though, her teacher saw Ruby stop and appear to speak with the angry people. Later, when Mrs. Hurley asked her student about the incident, Ruby explained. "I wasn't talking to them. I was just saying a prayer for them."[6]

Another time Mrs. Hurley observed the unruly crowd and later told Coles:

> I was standing in the classroom, looking out the window, and I saw Ruby coming down the street, with the federal marshals on both sides of her. The crowd was there, shouting as usual. A woman spat at Ruby but missed; Ruby smiled at her. A man shook his fist at her; Ruby smiled at him. Then she walked up the stairs, and she stopped and turned and smiled one more time! You know what she told one of the marshals? She told him she prays for those people, the ones in that mob, every night before she goes to sleep![7]

Dr. Coles, who is also a research psychiatrist, met with Ruby and her family during this demanding year and periodically in following years. He chronicled his observations in *Children of Crisis, Volume I* and *The Moral Life of Children*. Coles observed how acutely aware yet, for the most part, relatively unaffected Ruby was by the turmoil occurring around her.

As Coles sought to understand Ruby's reaction, she explained,

> They keep coming and saying the bad words, but my momma says they'll get tired after a while and then they'll stop coming. They'll stay home. The minister comes to our house and he said the same thing, and not to worry, and I don't. The minister said God is watching and He won't forget, because He never does. The minister says if I forgive the people, and smile at them, and pray for them, God will keep a good eye on everything and He'll be our protection.[8]

It is difficult to comprehend the simplicity of this child's heart in response to such a painful ordeal. As adults, when we suffer, it seems natural to lick our wounds and retreat into cynicism. Some of us may become angry that our rights have been violated and demand retribution. It seems an impossible task to love one's enemies. We can only love others with supernatural help.

That's what Ruby did; she responded with God's perspective. When we follow Christ's command as mentioned in Matthew 5:43–44 to "love [our] enemies and pray for those who persecute [us]," and seek His empowering to do so, we find we are able to do what seems humanly impossible. Ruby's actions show us the better way, the higher ground we can rise to, and the love of God lived out in action. Ruby showed us the power of what can happen when we follow the simple directives of God.

The individuals highlighted in this chapter illustrate how dramatically life can change for the better when we refuse to give into selfish fear and instead invest our lives for the good of others.

Living for Something Greater Than Ourselves

More than ever we live in fragile times where we face an uncertain future. Commentator Peggy Noonan warns:

Something's up. And deep down, where the body meets the soul, we are fearful. We fear, down so deep it hasn't even risen to the point of articulation, that with all our comforts and amusements, with all our toys and bells and whistles . . . we wonder if what we really have is . . . a first-class stateroom on the Titanic. Everything's wonderful, but a world is ending and we sense it.[9]

This uncertainty can lead us to being held hostage by fear. On the other hand, this uncertainty can be a catalyst to evaluate our lives to see what is truly worth living for. Our lives will be ultimately disappointing unless we live for something greater and bigger than ourselves.

Author and philosopher C.S. Lewis wrote, '

The principle runs through all life from top to bottom. Give up yourself, and you will find your real self. Lose your life and you will save it. . . . Keep nothing back. Nothing that you have not given away will ever really be yours. . . . Look for yourself, and you will find in the long run only hatred, loneliness, despair, rage, ruin, and decay. But look for Christ and you will find Him, and with Him everything else thrown in.[10]

When we choose to love and refuse to be bound by fear, little can stop us from having lives that make a difference for eternity. "It is through love that we enter the fullness of life and ultimately find happiness and fulfillment," John Powell explains.

We are not yet what we can be. Each moment and each

interaction can be an opportunity for good or for evil. Most of us have yet to see what our lives may look like and the impact we can make on our world when we are consumed by love. "We are half hearted creatures," Lewis noted, "fooling about with drink and sex and ambition when infinite joy is offered us, like an ignorant child who wants to go on making mud pies in the slum because he cannot imagine what is meant by the offer of a holiday at the sea. We are far too easily pleased."[11]

When we live our lives primarily for ourselves, like viewing the screen of a black-and-white television, the world takes on various shades of gray. We can see some distinction in the shadings from black to white, but there is no vibrancy. However, when we choose to become ambassadors of God's love, we find our lives suddenly radiate the full spectrum of the rainbow. In our own journey, Ray and I are forever thankful that we were given the opportunity to evaluate our lives and spend it for that which lasts. We are grateful that we faced our fears one by one and learned to walk in faith and love, trusting that God in His goodness had better things in store for us.

We invite you to join those who have loved without limits and given without restriction both their care and compassion. Let us move from fear to true, life-transforming love.

Notes

Chapter 2: Love: The Antidote to Fear

1. Jack Canfield and Mark Hansen, *Chicken Soup for the Soul* (Deerfield Beach, Fla.: Health Communications, 1993), 29.

2. On the Internet at www.larchecanada.org/frset1.html. Click "Jean Vanier"; then "Jean Vanier's letters to L'Arche"; then "July 2001." Accessed on 13 February 2002.

3. John Donne, *Devotions upon Emergent Occasions* (Ann Arbor, Mich.: Univ. of Michigan, 1959), 107–109.

4. K. Orth-Gomer and J. V. Johnson. "Social Network Interaction and Mortality: A Six Year Follow-Up Study of a Random Sample of the Swedish population," *Journal of Chronic Diseases* 40 (no. 10) (1987): 949–57; as cited in Dean Ornish, *Love and Survival* (New York: HarperCollins, 1998), 44.

5. B. S. Hanson, S. O. Isacsson, L. Janzon, and S. E. Lindell, "Social Network and Social Support Influence Mortality in Elderly Men," *American Journal of Epidemiology* 130 (no. 1) (1989): 100–111; as cited in Ornish, *Love and Survival,* 44.

6. "Immortal Beloveds," *Reader's Digest,* October 2001, 188.

7. Henri Nouwen, *Life of the Beloved* (New York: Crossroad, 1995), 57–59. Used by permission of The Crossroad Publishing Company.

8. Tony Campolo, *Let Me Tell You a Story* (Nashville: Word, 2000), 168.

9. Ibid., 169.

10. Dean Ornish, *Love and Survival* (New York: HarperCollins, 1998), 3.

Chapter 3: The Many Faces of Fear in Society

1. James Wooten, "The Face of AIDS," *World News Tonight,* ABC-TV, 6 July 2000. As cited on the Internet at www.abcnews.go.com/onair/worldnewstonight/ wnt000706_aidschild_feature.html; accessed on 7 June 2001.

2. Lynette Calmest, "The New Victims of Hate: Bias Crimes Hit America's Fastest Growing Ethnic Group," *Newsweek,* 6 November 2000, 61.

3. Ibid. The stories of John Lee and the fifty-year-old Laotian are both recounted in the *Newsweek* article "The New Victims of Hate," 61.

4. Barry Glassner, *The Culture of Fear* (New York: Basic, 1999), xxi. Glassner cites a study reported in Steen Stark, "Local News: The Biggest Scandal on TV," *Washington Monthly,* June 1997, 38–41.

5. Leonard Sweet, *A Cup of Coffee at the Soul Café* (Nashville: Broadman & Holman, 1998), 130.

6. Stephen James O'Meara "When the Wall (Street) Comes A Tumbling Down," *Odyssey,* 9 March 2000, 30.

7. As cited in Leonard Sweet, *A Cup of Coffee at the Soul Café,* 131.

8. "Hate Crime—He Wasn't Afraid," *Newsweek,* 15 October 2001, 8.

9. Ibid.

10. Henri J. M. Nouwen, *Lifesprings: Intimacy, Fecundity, and Ecstasy in Christian Perspective* (Garden City, N.Y.: Doubleday, 1986), 16.

11. Ibid., 16–17.

12. Susan Ager, "We the People: Isolated, Separate," Knight-Ridder/Tribune News Service, 11 August 1999.

13. Nouwen, *Lifespring,* 19.

14. As cited in "Are Americans Becoming Internet Slaves?" *USA Today* magazine, June 2000, 1.

15. As cited in Dean Ornish, *Love and Survival* (New York: HarperCollins, 1998), 101.

16. Ornish, *Love and Survival,* 12–13.

17. Tony Campolo, *Let Me Tell You a Story* (Nashville: Word, 2000), 43.

18. Charles Swindoll, *Dropping Your Guard* (Waco, Tex.: Word, 1987), 115.

Chapter 4: Components of Fear

1. Hadley Cantril, *The Invasion from Mars: A Study in the Psychology of Panic* (New York: Harper & Row, 1966) vi, 58. Originally published in 1940.

2. Ibid., 50.

3. Ibid., 53.

4. Ibid., 58.

5. National Institute of Mental Health, "Anxiety Disorders Research at the National Institute of Mental Health," Fact Sheet (Washington, D.C.: Government Printing Office, 1999), NIH publication no. 99-4504, updated 24 August 2000; as cited at www.nimh.nih.gov/publicat/anxresfact.cfm. Accessed on 27 February 2002.

6. Tony Campolo, *Let Me Tell You a Story* (Nashville: Word, 2000), 206–207.

7. Jerry Seinfeld, *I'm Telling You for the Last Time,* Universal Records, 1998.

8. Sharon Heller, *The Complete Idiot's Guide to Conquering Fear and Anxiety* (New York: Alpha, 1999), 3–4.

Chapter 5: The Battle for Love in Relationships

1. Philip Yancey, *Where Is God When It Hurts?* (Grand Rapids: Zondervan, 1988), n. p.

2. As retold by Michael O'Donnell, Bob and Charlotte Ann's daughter, during a personal conversation in Wheeling, Illinois.

3. As quoted in Leonard Sweet, *A Cup of Coffee at the Soul Café* (Nashville: Broadman & Holman, 1998), 30.

4. C. S. Lewis, *The Four Loves* (New York, Macmillan, 1960), 160.

5. Richard Selzer, *Mortal Lessons* (New York: Simon & Schuster, 1987), 45–47. Copyright © 1974, 1975, 1976, 1987 by Richard Selzer. Reprinted by permission of George Borchardt, Inc., for the author.

6. John Powell, *Unconditional Love* (Allen, Tex.: Tabor, 1978), 10.

7. Joe Kohut, *The Little Book of Phobias,* (Philadelphia: Running Press, 1994), 49.

8. Henri Nouwen, *Lifesprings* (Garden City, N.Y.: Doubleday, 1986), 15.

9. Ibid., 30.

10. Clyde Reid, *Celebrate the Temporary* (New York: Harper & Row, 1972), 43.

11. Ibid.

12. Frank Donnelly as cited in Tim Hansel, *You Gotta Keep Dancin'*, (Wheaton, Ill.: Victor, 1992), 63.

13. G. W. Target, *The Window and Other Essays* (Nampa, Idaho: Pacific Press, 1973), 5–7. Used by permission of Pacific Press, P.O. Box 5353, Nampa, Idaho 83653.

14. Daphne Rose Kingma, *The Book of Love* (Berkeley, Calif.: Conari Books, 2001), 77.

Chapter 6: The Major Relational Fears

1. Sharon Heller, *The Complete Idiot's Guide to Conquering Fear and Anxiety* (New York: Alpha, 1999), 195.

2. Jeffrey Kluger, "Fear Not!" *Time,* 2 April 2001, 58.

3. Sheldon Kopp, *Raise Your Right Hand against Fear* (Minneapolis: CompCare, 1988), 97–98.

4. Peter G. Van Breeman, *Called by Name* (Denville, N.J.: Doubleday, 1991), 39; as cited in Brennan Manning, *Abba's Child* (Colorado Springs: NavPress, 1994), 136.

5. Though a pseudonym, "Nathan" is an actual person Nancy counseled (not a composite); some details have been changed to protect his identity.

6. John Bradshaw, *Bradshaw on: The Family* (Deerfield Beach, Fla.: Health Communications, 1988), 3.

7. Ibid., 3.

8. Ernest Becker, *Denial of Death* (New York: Simon & Schuster, 1973), xii.

9. Iris Murdoch, *The Nice and the Good* (New York: Penguin, 1978), 315; also in Manning, *Abba's Child,* 150.

Chapter 7: Steps in Overcoming Our Fears

1. Adapted from Sharon Heller, *The Complete Idiot's Guide to Overcoming Fear and Anxiety* (New York: Alpha, 1999), 170.

2. As cited in Leonard Pitts Jr., "Depth of Character Develops When Facing Failure," Knight-Ridder News Service, 9 May 1997.

3. Jeffrey Kluger, "Fear Not!" *Time,* 2 April 2001, 62.

4. Margery Williams, *The Velveteen Rabbit* (New York: Avon 1975), 16–17.

5. H. Norman Wright, *Afraid No More* (Wheaton, Ill.: Tyndale, 1989), 75–76.

6. See, for example, Jeremiah 29:11; Romans 8:28; 1 Thessalonians 2:12; 1 Peter 5:10.

7. Ernest Gordon, *Through the Valley of the Kwai* (New York: Harper & Brothers, 1962), 102–105.

Chapter 8: Fear and Control

1. David A. Katerndahl, "Relationship Between Panic Attacks and Health Locus of Control," *Journal of Family Practice* 32, no. 4 (April 1991): 391.

2. John A. Astin et. al., "Sense of Control and Adjustment to Breast Cancer," *Behavioral Medicine* 25, no. 3 (Fall, 1999): 101.

3. David G. Myers, *The Pursuit of Happiness* (New York: Morrow, 1992), 113–16.

4. Daniel Goleman, *Emotional Intelligence* (New York: Bantam, 1996), 80–81.

5. Les Parrott III, *The Control Freak* (Wheaton, Ill.: Tyndale, 2000), 43.

6. Elizabeth Brenner, *Winning by Letting Go, Control Without Compulsion, Surrender Without Defeat* (New York: Harcourt, Brace, Jovanovich, 1985), 32.

7. Thomas McCann, *An American Company: The Story of the United Fruit Company* (New York: Crown, 1976), 125–26.

8. Ibid., 127.

9. Michael MacCoby, "Narcissistic Leaders: The Incredible Pros, the Inevitable Cons," *Harvard Business Review,* January–February 2000.

10. Os Guinness, *The Call* (Nashville: Word, 1998), 88.

Chapter 9: When Anger Supercharges Our Fears

1. C. Leslie Charles, *Why Is Everyone So Cranky?* (New York: Hyperion, 1999), 369, 8.

2. Leon James and Diane Nahl, *Road Rage and Aggressive Driving* (New York: Prometheus, 2000), 48.

3. E. B. Ebbesen, B. Duncan, and V. J. Konecni, "Effects of Content of Verbal Aggression on Future Verbal Aggression: A Field Experiment," *Journal of Experimental Social Psychology* 11 (1975): 192–204; as cited in David Nyers, *Discovering Psychology* (New York: Worth, 1990), 345.

Chapter 11: Love That Overcomes

1. "Courage in the Air," *Newsweek. Commemorative Issue,* Fall 2001, 33–34.

2. Jess Moody, as cited in Lloyd Core, ed., *Quote Unquote,* (Wheaton, Ill.: Victor, 1977), 66.

3. Mother Teresa of Calcutta, *No Greater Love* (Novato, Calif.: New World, 1997), 25.

4. Patrice O'Shaughnessy, "Mother's Teresa Journey of Love Ends," *New York Daily News,* 13 September 1997.

5. "Living Out Our Spirituality," on the Internet at www.larchecanada.org. Accessed on 13 February 2002.

6. Robert Coles, "The Inexplicable Prayers of Ruby Bridges," *Christianity Today,* 9 August 1985, 19.

7. Robert Coles, *The Moral Life of Children* (New York: Atlantic Monthly, 1986), 22–27.

8. Ibid., 24.

9. Peggy Noonan, "There Is No Time, There Will Be Time," 30 November 1998, *Forbes ASAP* (special issue: "Fifty-Seven Minds on Time"), 80–81.

10. C. S. Lewis, *Mere Christianity* (New York: Macmillan, 1960), 190.

11. C. S. Lewis, *The Weight of Glory and Other Addresses* (New York: Simon & Schuster, 1980), 26.